TAKING A KNEE, TAKING A STAND

TAKING A KNEE, TAKING A STAND

African American Athletes and the Fight for Social Justice

BOB SCHRON

Foreword by Devin McCourty

imagine!

An Imagine Book
Published by Charlesbridge
85 Main Street
Watertown, MA 02472
(617) 926-0329
www.imaginebooks.net

Interior design by Jeff Miller
Jacket design by LMA Communications

Library of Congress Cataloging-in-Publication Data
Names: Schron, Bob, author.
Title: Taking a knee, taking a stand : African American athletes and the fight for social justice/ Bob Schron.
Description: Watertown, MA : Charlesbridge, 2020. | Summary: "A decade-by-decade account of
    African American athlete activism told through the stories of prominent athletes who fought for
    racial or gender equality." — Provided by publisher.
Identifiers: LCCN 2019020909 (print) | LCCN 2019981485 (ebook)
| ISBN 9781623545376 (hard cover)
| ISBN 9781632892188 (ebook)
Subjects: LCSH: African American athletes—Political activity—History. | African American political
    activists. | Racism—United States—History.
Classification: LCC GV706.32 .S37 2020 (print) | LCC GV706.32 (ebook) |
    DDC 796.08996—dc23
LC record available at https://lccn.loc.gov/2019020909
LC ebook record available at https://lccn.loc.gov/2019981485

Printed in Singapore
(hc) 10 9 8 7 6 5 4 3 2 1

CONTENTS

FOREWORD

AM HONORED to be part of an American sports tradition that goes back over a hundred years. It is a tradition that shows how athletes can—through talent, hard work, and opportunity—get better and better at what we do, and build on the achievements of the great athletes who came before us.

I am proud too of my record with the New England Patriots, and honored to be a captain of one of the iconic franchises in the history of sports. Since I've played for the Patriots, we have won three Super Bowl titles. We are proud of our place in the region and happy to know we have given back to the community, on and off the field.

But I'm also deeply aware of my responsibility as a professional athlete. Sports plays a massive role in our culture, and we are living through a time of divisiveness and unfairness. It is important to understand that we are at a turning point in the fight for social justice. It is undeniable that people in certain segments of the country, specifically people of color, continue to be treated unjustly. And this injustice has intensified since the election of 2016.

So how does a man or woman of principle handle things? I'm a Christian, and after that election I talked to our chaplain, who said it best: "We just have to pray for the leadership of our country, whether you agree with it or disagree with it; you pray for the leadership and you believe there's a way everything will be all right. Pray on it and hope everything works out well and believe in God."

Our chaplain was right—leadership is key. And while I pray for national leadership, I also recognize that God calls those of us with influence and opportunity to also lead. Because as professional athletes and African Americans, there is another tradition we are part of. When I consider athletes like Bill Russell or the NFL great Jim Brown, I see men who would never back down from challenging injustice, even when their stand wreaked havoc with their personal lives. More and more of us see their example of how we can utilize the platform sports gives us to foster meaningful change.

Taking a Knee, Taking a Stand tells the stories of Russell, Brown, Muhammad Ali, Wilma Rudolph, and other male and female athletes who, over the last hundred years or so, have battled racism and discrimination. Their history helps today's athletes take the long view on our social mission. Here we are, two decades into a new century, and we continue to witness how the roots of violence that our past heroes worked so hard to defeat have not been eradicated. Injustice remains. We still live with the same social issues that have plagued our country for generations. And today's athletes have to decide: Do I sit on the sideline and wait for others to step up, or do I become part of the solution?

We have heard the false narratives aimed at those of us who play at the highest level. *Don't mix sports and politics. Shut up and dribble. Just play football.* Professional athletes have heard these phrases over and over. But athletes are members of society with voices that have a wide reach and an opportunity to create real change. I'm excited to be a part of this change because I think it is more valuable than anything I could accomplish on the football field.

When senseless things happen, resistance is a matter of both faith and action. If I may make a personal statement: My mom, Phyllis McCourty, a single mother and a nurse, raised my twin brother, Jason, and me after our father died when we were very young. She worked endless hours so we could attend private school. We lived in a trailer for part of that time, but her sacrifice allowed us to pursue our dream. With her help, I went to Rutgers University, where I was fortunate enough to earn two academic Big East designations and went on to receive a degree in sociology. My mom's example showed me how to overcome odds. To develop steely resiliency.

My mom displayed faith and action. Her platform was her family, and she used it. It wasn't easy, but she did it. She was, for me personally, heroic. So now it's my turn. How do I overturn those false narratives? How do I help correct misunderstandings about patriotism and sports and politics that extend as far as the Oval Office? How can I use my influence to change policy and legislation, to improve communities and address problems like mass incarceration?

These are hard questions. And there are risks. When an athlete of conscience like Colin Kaepernick chose to take a highly unpopular stand against injustice, he paid a heavy price. He lost the ability to play his sport during crucial years at the heart of his career. It was a travesty not to see him back in the league. Those of us who have played against him know he has the kind of talent that should have made him an obvious choice for any number of NFL teams—but he was consistently bypassed.

I see Kaepernick as an awesome human being. For what he stands for. And for what he did. In this latest movement of athletes fighting for justice, he was the first to step out on a ledge. He is part of that long tradition of dissent going back to Jackie Robinson and Ali, to Tommie Smith and

John Carlos. This tradition has inspired NFL players, and athletes from other sports, to search for positive ways of building on the awareness that Kaepernick's brave action has generated.

The NFL Players Coalition is a good example of such positive action. Founded in 2017 by Anquan Boldin and Malcolm Jenkins, the organization has a collective goal of making an impact on social justice and racial equality at the federal, state, and local levels through advocacy, awareness, education, and allocation of resources. I am proud to be on the Coalition's Task Force.

The Players Coalition is changing lives by connecting with communities and getting involved with legislation to change policies. We are attacking issues this country has endured for generations, and I've learned that it's not easy. But along with other members of the Task Force, I am learning to navigate issues that generally make others uncomfortable. Issues like holding police accountable. Combating racial bias. But when tough decisions need to be made, I remember a phrase I heard long ago: *Leaders must be comfortable being uncomfortable.*

The stories in this book are stories of African American athletes who made a difference. Yes, they were uncomfortable. Yes, they often suffered setbacks for standing up for their beliefs. But like my mom they had steely resiliency. They set the example. They were leaders.

Devin McCourty

INTRODUCTION

AMERICA LOVES ITS SPORTS. We love the highs of victory and the lows of defeat. The grace, intensity, and drama. The meritocracy of athletic competition: here, for once, is an arena where the best generally triumph. And many of us love the escape that sports offer—from workday stress to family tension to partisan politics. A football game delivers an emotionally unambiguous experience: This is my team. I identify with it. I celebrate when it wins and mourn when it loses.

And then there are the stars of the sports world. Our twenty-first-century obsession with celebrity, media, and instant communication has given sports figures fame and treasure beyond what anyone could have imagined a generation ago. Massive salaries, huge endorsement opportunities, global recognition. Yet these remarkably talented and famous men and women are close to us. We feel an intimacy, as if they are our friends. Our representatives. Not only do we want them to perform beautifully and to win, we want to *like* them. We want to feel as if we are part of their community.

This recognition and intimacy give the greatest of our athletes an awe-inspiring platform. Their influence is broad and deep. Millions of people *attend* to LeBron James and Serena Williams. They *listen* to Magic Johnson and Colin Kaepernick. And this mass attention affords those athletes a unique opportunity to shape our culture and our politics.

And let's make no mistake: sports is political. There are those who would tell us that athletes should keep their mouths shut and play ball—that they are simply entertainers. "NFL players are at it again," President Donald Trump tweeted in 2018. "Taking a knee when they should be standing proudly for the National Anthem." Earlier he had called those who kneel during the playing of the national anthem before football games "sons of bitches" and said that if they won't stand during the anthem, they should be fired. Of course, there are racial undertones to Trump's disrespect. Historically, and especially since 2016, when Colin Kaepernick took a knee during the anthem prior to an NFL preseason game, the protests that Trump hates so much have been almost exclusively by African Americans who made the risky decision to use their platform to draw attention to racism.

"I am not going to stand up to show pride in a flag for a country that oppresses black people and people of color," Kaepernick said after that first protest. "To me, this is bigger than football, and it would be selfish on my part to look the other way. There are bodies in the street and people getting paid leave and getting away with murder."

Kaepernick's reference to black bodies and police cover-ups was pointed. It was a tough message, a raw message, delivered after two tragic years of high-profile police killings of unarmed black men, from Michael Brown in Ferguson, Missouri, in the summer of 2014 to Alton Sterling and Philando Castile in the summer of 2016—and many since. And Kaepernick has paid for being so outspoken. In spite of his obvious talent and leadership abilities, as well as his relative youth, he has not worked in the NFL since the end of the 2016 season. In November 2017, two months

San Francisco 49ers quarterback Colin Kaepernick (right) and free safety Eric Reid kneel during the national anthem before an NFL game between the 49ers and the Los Angeles Rams in 2016.

after Trump's incendiary "fire them" statement, Kaepernick filed a collusion grievance against the NFL, accusing owners of working together to keep him out of professional football.

Kaepernick's protest is part of a tradition. It is a *necessary* tradition, with roots in pre-Civil War slavery revolts and early twentieth-century activism against the steady erosion of what little gains African Americans had made during Reconstruction. The tradition includes heavyweight boxer Jack Johnson's refusal to observe the rules of so-called polite society even though he was consistently harassed, berated, and imprisoned because of his race. It is a tradition that includes the sporting achievements and political bravery of those African American athletes, most of them from the South, who competed and stood up for themselves and their communities during the dark days of Jim Crow: Jesse Owens, Joe Louis, Jackie Robinson, Wilma Rudolph, and countless others whose names are less well known.

It is a civil rights tradition of women and men who, in the face of antagonism from the white establishment, spoke and acted out of conscience, even though it harmed their careers—Muhammad Ali, Tommie

Smith and John Carlos, Mahmoud Abdul-Rauf. And it is a tradition that has been revitalized in the twenty-first century not just by the NFL protesters, but by confident, outspoken athletes from the NBA to the Women's Tennis Association (WTA).

These athletes are American heroes. In the fullest sense. They have refused to be intimidated. In the context of their times, which varied as the decades passed, they succeeded in spite of hardships and hatreds that, throughout the last hundred years and longer, have modulated in form and intensity but never gone away. Their heroism—and the heroism of so many who will remain unremembered—are more than athletic. Such heroism is cultural. It is political.

Because of this tradition of activism and protest, athletes now occasionally have more power than politicians. Whether it is the Missouri college football team protesting the university's handling of racial tensions on campus, or LeBron James and fellow NBA players speaking out at the ESPY Awards, or Kareem Abdul-Jabbar leading the opposition to Donald Trump's proposal to ban Muslims from coming to the United States, black athletes recognize the power of their platform and feel empowered to speak out on social and political issues. And their message is clear: Racism is not dead. It remains a current problem. It is the responsibility of all Americans to admit this and to work to defeat it.

President Barack Obama, when talking about race, liked to quote the novelist William Faulkner: "The past isn't dead. It isn't even past." American history is harsh and painful, especially for African Americans, and it is tempting for white Americans to assume that what caused that pain is long gone. But as Faulkner's words remind us, history is a living force that carries forward. And the pain remains, in the form of discrimination, denial, and double standards. In mass incarceration and the extrajudicial killings of young black men. Past progress is welcome, but it cannot—must not—rule out the continued pursuit of justice. In fact, the past must *inform* the present. Otherwise, the legacy of denial will never be overcome.

The great basketball player Bill Russell put it best: "You only register progress by how far you have to go."

Taking a Knee, Taking a Stand celebrates these African American heroes for their athletic greatness, for the bravery and intelligence of their activism, and for their leadership. It is a book about the past *and* the present, a commemoration of some of the greatest athletes in the history of American sports, who also had the courage and determination to take a stand against racism—at times when it felt as if the whole country were against them. It is about African American women and men who became leaders—many reluctantly—because they recognized that their sporting prowess gave them a platform. This leadership took many forms. Sometimes it was quiet and subtle, as when Joe Louis worked behind the scenes to battle bigotry in a segregated US Army. Other times, it was loud and abrasive, as when Muhammad Ali publicly called out his country for requiring him to fight in a war that he considered immoral.

But *Taking a Knee, Taking a Stand* also looks ahead. Past leadership enables present activism, which leads to future progress. The heroes profiled in this book encourage today's African American athletes to continue what Obama called "the long march of those who come before us." They help all Americans recognize that history is dynamic and incremental. That those who fail to learn from the past are destined to repeat its mistakes.

Another way of describing the connectedness of past and present activism is to say that it is *intersectional*. The race, class, sexuality, religion, and gender of any individual or group cannot be separated from each other. They overlap and create, in a society that often lacks respect for those who are different, multiple avenues of discrimination. The journey of African American athlete activism over the last hundred years has been a gradual awakening of black male awareness to the challenges of other forms of bigotry: against all people of color, against women, religious groups, the lesbian, gay, bisexual, and transgender (LGBTQ) community, and those with physical disabilities.

So this book tells the stories not just of Jackie Robinson and Bill Russell and LeBron James, but of tennis stars Venus Williams and Althea Gibson and of Wilma Rudolph, the remarkable track star who overcame poverty and physical disability to become the first American woman to win three gold medals in a single Olympics. Rudolph's courage in facing down Jim Crow attitudes in her hometown of Clarksville, Tennessee, was as stirring an example of leadership under pressure as you will find.

History lives. Black Lives Matter takes up the mantle of the sixties civil rights movement. Today's athletes—more prosperous and more secure than their forebears—stand on the shoulders of the giants of the past. Jackie Robinson's breaking of the baseball color line was as vital to the civil rights movement as *Brown v. Board of Education*, just as Kareem Abdul-Jabbar's challenges to the white establishment support progressive causes seventy years after Robinson, and Venus Williams's actions are aimed at equal pay for women and the rights of working mothers.

But let's not forget that these great athlete activists also happened to be the best in the world at their day jobs. Yes, they were political giants, but they also changed their sports forever on the field and the court, in the ring and the stadium. Louis, Robinson, Bill Russell in basketball, and Jim Brown in football were the kings of their professions, and Serena Williams remains the queen of her sport, tennis. They dominated and innovated. Tommie Smith and John Carlos will always be remembered for raising their fists on the podium during the national anthem after they had won the gold and bronze medals, respectively, in the 200-meter event at the 1968 Olympics. But their performances in that race were *dazzling*. Muhammad Ali, though he was robbed of the peak years of his boxing life by a government that refused to accept his intersectional protest to the Vietnam War, still put together a career that proved he was, by far, the greatest boxer, if not the greatest athlete, of all time.

The stories in this book, then, are both inspirational and aspirational. They honor the achievements of these great athletes, but stay mindful of the unnamed many who were denied their dreams because of the legal, cultural, and institutional legacy of racism. They further honor the women and men, white and black, who—though not central figures in this book—nevertheless played key roles in supporting the cause of justice. The sociologist Dr. Harry Edwards of San Jose State mentored Tommie Smith and John Carlos, gave forthright and unflinching advice about race to Major League Baseball and the San Francisco 49ers, and, a half-century after the 1968 Olympics, counseled Colin Kaepernick. Billie Jean King was one of the greatest tennis players of all time, yet she struggled while on top of the tennis world with the establishment's belief that women players should not receive equal pay. Then, when her sexuality was publicized in 1981 against her will, she lost all of her endorsement deals. Yet discrimination made her more determined, and her crusade for equality never faltered.

No one fights alone. Within the broad tradition of African American athlete activism are specific lines of influence. In the tennis world, Althea Gibson inspired Arthur Ashe, who inspired Venus and Serena Williams. Bill Russell inspired Kareem Abdul-Jabbar, who inspired LeBron James. Jackie Robinson and Muhammad Ali . . . well, they inspired *everyone*.

This is how leadership works. This is how history works. Individual excellence and individual bravery must take their place in the collective striving for fairness. And in time, the reverberations of the contributions of these athletes, of their courage to fight for what is right, are felt at the highest levels of politics: Look at President Bill Clinton's friendship with Magic Johnson, Obama's admiration of Muhammad Ali, and South African president Nelson Mandela's high regard for Arthur Ashe. There will always be people who revile those with the courage to take a knee. But history vindicates the honest pursuit of justice and the sacrifice of taking a stand. Only in this way will the long march for equality continue.

SETTING THE STAGE FOR ACTIVISM
Jesse Owens and Joe Louis

1

THE WINNERS' PODIUM at the Olympics is one of the world's most powerful platforms. It symbolizes victory, patriotism, and peak personal performance. It captures moments, enhanced by precious metals and national anthems, that are profoundly emotional and globally viewed. And, under certain circumstances, it yields iconic images that rise above the world of sports and reverberate in history.

One such moment occurred after Jesse Owens won the long jump final in the 1936 Summer Olympics in Berlin, the second of four gold medals he would win there. These were the Games that Adolf Hitler assumed would showcase what he believed was Germany's racial superiority. The day before, however, after Owens won the 100-meter dash with a record-setting performance, Hitler famously left the stadium without shaking his hand—an assumed snub that made the front pages of all major American newspapers. Owens's performance, the headlines trumpeted, had exposed Hitler's delusional claims; overnight, the track star became an American hero.

After winning the gold medal and setting a world record in the long jump at the 1936 Summer Olympics in Berlin, Jesse Owens salutes the American flag while surrounded by athletes and officials making the Nazi salute.

Photographs of Owens's achievements were wired throughout the world, including one of him on the podium after his long jump victory, respectfully saluting while German officials and silver medalist Luz Long *sieg heil*ed an absent Führer—Hitler had left the stadium yet again. The photo added visual potency to the news of his success: the victor's laurels encircling his head, the winner's bouquet in the crook of his left arm, "USA" emblazoned across his sweatshirt. It was, and remains, an image of individual heroism rising above the mindlessness of fascist subservience.

But history is all about context, and the decades that followed would add nuance to this famous image, as well as enhance our understanding of how to interpret Owens's success, not only in terms of sports, but also within the ongoing historical conversation about race in America. Thirty-two years later, at the 1968 Summer Olympics in Mexico City, Tommie Smith and John Carlos—African American sprinters who were extend-

A very different salute: at the medals ceremony for the 200-meter run at the 1968 Summer Olympics in Mexico City, Tommie Smith (center) and John Carlos raise their gloved fists in protest against racism and social injustice in the US and throughout the world. Peter Norman (left), who took the silver medal, would be poorly treated upon his return to his native Australia after supporting Smith and Carlos.

ing the tradition of Olympic success that Owens initiated—would offer the world an altogether different podium salute.

The Black Power fists that Smith and Carlos raised following their gold- and bronze-medal performances in the 200-meter sprint—while the American national anthem played—had been calmly and carefully considered by these athletes. These gestures were anything but subservient. They were intelligently defiant. The black gloves expressed African American strength and unity. The men also wore black socks and no shoes to symbolize African American poverty, beads to honor the memory of lynching victims, and buttons of the Olympic Project for Human Rights (OPHR), which was working to combat racial segregation in the United States, South Africa, and elsewhere.

Sadly and predictably, the public response to this bold protest was the opposite of what it had been for Owens. International Olympic Committee (IOC) president Avery Brundage demanded that both runners be suspended and moved from the Olympic Village. The American press was scathing. Brent Musburger, at the time a columnist for the *Chicago*

American newspaper, wrote that Smith and Carlos "looked like a couple of black-skinned storm troopers," an epithet not just explicitly racist but obscene in its comparison of the runners with Nazis. (One of the many ironies of this incident, which will be explored in more detail later in this book, is that Brundage, an "America Firster" and president of the US Olympic Committee (USOC) during the Berlin Games, had opposed a potential US boycott of the Olympics in 1936 and also, under pressure by his Nazi hosts, had prevented two Jewish runners on the American track team from participating in the finals of the 4 × 100 relay. Smith and Carlos raising their fists in anger and righteousness had enraged Brundage, but he had no problem with Nazi salutes to Hitler.)

Thus, history moves. What then to make of Owens? The conventional story is that this grandson of slaves singlehandedly defeated the Nazi myth of Aryan supremacy. But Owens himself was aware that this narrative was incomplete. "When I came back to my native country," he said, "after all the stories about Hitler, I couldn't ride in the front of the bus. I had to go to the back door. I couldn't live where I wanted. I wasn't invited to shake hands with Hitler, but I wasn't invited to the White House to shake hands with the president, either."

In Germany, Owens had stayed in the same hotels as the white members of the American team. When he returned to the United States, he was thrown a ticker-tape parade in Manhattan, but afterward, he was not allowed through the main doors of the Waldorf Astoria hotel; he had to take the freight elevator to reach a reception given in *his* honor. This was the reality of institutionalized American racism. This was Jim Crow personified.

Men and women must live their lives and fight injustice in ways that make sense for their time. Like the celebrated boxer Joe Louis, another African American sports superstar of the thirties, Owens had to negotiate his success and fame in light of racist hatreds that were so ingrained in American culture that they were enshrined in mainstream customs and attitudes, in the media, in the country's institutions, and in its laws. And let's not forget that this occurred during the Great Depression, when financial hardship was deep and extensive in America, intensifying the suffering that segregation imposed on African Americans.

Louis and Owens were almost exact contemporaries, with remarkably similar backgrounds—both born and raised in Alabama, a year apart; both sons of sharecropping parents whose own parents had been slaves and who moved north (to Detroit and Cleveland, respectively) in the first wave of the Great Migration of African Americans after World War I. As children, both men had been surrounded by the pathological racism of the Deep South and its worst excesses: lynchings, everyday humiliations, the de facto slavery of black men and women who were arrested for vagrancy and then indentured to corporations like US Steel, and even the violent predations of the Ku Klux Klan (KKK) (Louis's family had moved to Detroit after being threatened by the Klan).

Like Owens, Joe Louis was to become a national symbol of anti-Nazi resistance. On June 19, 1936, just weeks before Owens's Olympic triumphs, Louis fought the German Max Schmeling, former world heavyweight champion, in Yankee Stadium. Schmeling upset the heavily favored American with a stunning knockout in twelve rounds, after which Hitler sent Schmeling's wife flowers and a message: "For the wonderful victory of your husband, our greatest German boxer, I must congratulate you with all my heart." In a world increasingly divided along racial and nationalistic lines, Louis's defeat produced a resounding effect.

The rematch, which would occur two years later, after Louis had won the heavyweight belt from James Braddock, became a national obsession. The Nazi propaganda machine exploited Schmeling to the fullest (against his wishes, by the way). President Franklin Delano Roosevelt invited Louis to the White House (Owens must have bristled), where he told him, "Joe, we need muscles like yours to beat Germany." Seventy million people listened to Clem McCarthy's call of the fight on the radio. Louis was

Joe Louis waits in a neutral corner after knocking down German heavyweight Max Schmeling during their fight in Yankee Stadium on June 22, 1938.

ruthlessly effective, beating Schmeling so badly that the fight was called before the end of the first round. Louis—and America—were vindicated.

In the words of boxing writer Tim Smith, Louis's victory allowed the country to see African Americans as *Americans*. And there is no denying the positive impact the victory had on the black community, from Arkansas to Harlem. "Some black woman's son was the strongest man in the world," poet Maya Angelou said. The comedian and activist Dick Gregory put it this way: "Draw a couple of parallel lines through history. On one side, you had the horse; then the automobile; then the airplane; and then the rocket. With Joe's victory, for us, looking back, you had a reason to hope: you had Lincoln; you had Joe Louis and Sugar Ray Robinson; you had Emmett Till; you had Rosa Parks; and then Dr. King. Before that fight, grandmothers got down on their knees and prayed. And when we won, everyone walked a little bit straighter."

But as with Owens, there is more to the narrative than what showed on the surface. "The problem of the twentieth century," W. E. B. DuBois had written in 1903, "is the color line." That line was as sharply drawn as ever in the thirties, and crossing it was no simple matter, even for the most privileged. Louis would later say he should have been more of an activist. Yet at the end of his life, he concluded, "I did the best I could with what I had." That was true. And his best was a great deal.

As the observations of Angelou and Gregory imply, Owens and Louis were activists by virtue of their achievements. The constraints on outspokenness were overwhelming. Had either been more public about the racism they experienced day to day, the result would likely have been counterproductive. Yet during the civil rights campaigns of the sixties, the two men were sometimes called Uncle Toms—unthinking criticism that missed an essential point: What these men did was truly heroic, in the sense that their achievements were *empowering*—for all Americans, but particularly for African Americans.

Louis's career developed in the shadow of Jack Johnson, and his public behavior must be considered in light of his predecessor's legacy. The "Galveston Giant," as Johnson was called, was the first African American heavyweight champion of the world, reigning from 1908 to 1915, a period of rising racism brought on by the failure of Reconstruction and resistance to the efforts of African Americans to cross the color line. Johnson's most profound battles were against attempts to take his title from him, and in particular the overtly racist search for a "Great White Hope." After Johnson had won the world crown, the author Jack London pleaded with former champion Jim Jeffries to come out of retirement and "remove that golden smile from Jack Johnson's face . . . the white man must be rescued." Jeffries complied, or tried to, and when the fight was set for July 4,

1910, the *New York Times* commented, "If the black man wins, thousands and thousands of his ignorant brothers will misinterpret his victory as justifying claims to much more than mere physical equality with their white neighbors."

Johnson beat Jeffries convincingly, and white Americans were not happy. Race riots broke out from Los Angeles to New York, African Americans were lynched and gunned down, and hundreds were injured. Johnson remained defiant. Arrogant and openly rebellious, he refused to play by the rules of the white establishment, dating white women, opening an integrated nightclub, recklessly driving expensive cars, and partying wildly. In 1912, he was arrested for violating the Mann Act (which outlawed "transporting a woman across state lines for immoral purposes"), and the following year, he was convicted by an all-white jury in the court of Judge Kenesaw Mountain Landis, the future baseball commissioner notorious for maintaining the color line in the major leagues until his death in 1944. After the conviction, Johnson fled to Europe and then Mexico City, staying away from the United States for seven years while he denounced racism and white supremacy.

In the sixties, Johnson would become a hero to African American activists and artists, including jazz legend Miles Davis, whose *Tribute to Jack Johnson* is one of his greatest recordings. But in the thirties, with Jim Crow still in effect and the hatred unleashed in response to Johnson's behavior still fresh and active in the culture, a quiet, humble man like Joe Louis would react to the racial climate in a very different way. Starting with his debut at the age of seventeen, he established himself as a Golden Gloves, Amateur Athletic Union (AAU), and then professional champion, sweeping through the heavyweight ranks and defeating the top fighters of the day, including Primo Carnera, Billy Conn, and Jersey Joe Walcott. But Louis remained guarded, maintaining a cautious inner space, where the public and media could not reach him.

This strategy was partly political, partly temperamental, and partly driven by economic necessity. Louis's managers believed that if he slipped up, the reactionary response that followed Johnson's success would repeat itself, cutting Louis off from his livelihood, his ambition, and his ability to realize a dream that would inspire African Americans all over the continent. Remember that in the thirties, boxing rivaled baseball as America's most popular sport. During the Great Depression, its ferocity and mano a mano competitiveness appealed to people who were besieged by economic hardship. The rise of radio also made the sport accessible to a huge national audience. Yet in a failing economy, purses remained small, and popularity was no guarantee of financial success.

And white supremacists were still watching closely. Ahead of Louis's 1935 victory over Max Baer, legendary sportswriter Shirley Povich observed, "They say Baer will surpass himself in the knowledge that he is the lone white hope for the defense of Nordic superiority in the prize ring." (It should be pointed out that later, Povich would champion the cause of integration, publicly and repeatedly chastising the Washington Redskins for having an all-white football team as late as 1962.)

In Louis's quest for boxing immortality, he was skillfully supported early in his career in two essential ways: by his managers, John Boxborough and Julian Black, and by his trainer, Jack Blackburn. All three were African Americans. In the complex, renegade world of prizefighting, all had succeeded in the sport by operating—and surviving—inside and outside the law. Boxborough and Black were racketeers; Blackburn had served time in prison for manslaughter. But there was no doubting their brilliance. Many boxing experts rank Blackburn the equal of the greatest trainers in the sport—Angelo Dundee, Eddie Fuchs, and Ray Arcel. He was an expert not just in the art and science of boxing, but in the social psychology of his boxer's situation: he understood how vital it was for Louis to present an image that would be acceptable to a white audience, including the corporate interests backing the sport, such as Ford, where Louis had once worked in the automobile parts factory.

So Louis and his management pursued the same strategy that Branch Rickey would follow when he and Jackie Robinson successfully integrated baseball in the following decade. Indeed, it was the only way to proceed, given the starkness of the color line. Louis was reticent in public. He kept a low profile. He never gloated over an opponent. He lived and fought cleanly.

Jesse Owens came to a comparable strategy by a different route. His passion for running had begun in the fields of Alabama. After moving to Cleveland with his family in the early twenties, Owens, with his natural speed and balance, caught the attention of Charles Riley, the first in a series of coaches to help Owens rescue himself from a life of stark poverty. By the time he reached high school, he was holding his own on the track against Olympic-standard athletes, leading to his enrollment in Ohio State, where he would be coached to greatness by Larry Snyder, one of the few US college coaches who would allow black athletes to compete.

Owens achieved eminence and fame at Ohio State, but during his time there, he was constantly reminded of the color line. At the Big Ten Championships in Ann Arbor, Michigan, in 1935, he set four world records, foreshadowing his Olympic dominance the following year. Owens said that he ran as if the track were a hot stove and he was doing his best not to get burned. But his pride was being burned in other ways. Although he was the first black captain of the Ohio State track team, every day he was made aware of his second-class status as an American citizen. He lived in substandard, segregated housing at the university. He had to shower separately from his teammates and stay in black-only hotels when the team traveled. He was judged one way as an athlete and another way as a man.

Many African Americans had urged Owens to bypass the Ann Arbor meet, just as members of the AAU would encourage him to boycott the

1936 Games because of the Nazis' Nuremberg Laws, which stripped German Jews of their citizenship rights and equal treatment under the law (ultimately, the AAU would narrowly vote to attend). This activism was stoked by a racist media, which endorsed the belief of US Olympic coach Dean Cromwell when he said that "the Negro athlete excels because he is closer to the primitive than the white athlete. It was not so long ago that his ability to sprint and jump was a life-and-death matter to him in the jungle. His muscles are pliable and his easygoing disposition is a valuable aid to the mental and physical relaxation that a runner and jumper must have."

Cromwell's comments were just one of a range of erroneous and insidious explanations for black sporting success that must have cut Owens and other African American athletes to the quick. Close inspection of the newspaper coverage of Owens's Olympic success—so celebratory on the surface—reveals a not-so-subtle racism lying beneath. After Owens's performance leading the American 4 × 100 relay team to victory by an amazing 15 meters, the Nazi Party newspaper *Der Angriff* labeled the runners "Black Auxiliaries." But American newspaper accounts could be equally demeaning: sportswriter Grantland Rice, for example, described the victory as a "darktown parade."

With a few exceptions, including (of course) writers for the African American newspapers of the time, American sportswriters in the thirties (an exclusively male club) publicly expressed themselves in line with the prejudice of the day. They freely utilized "alliterative racial and jungle nicknames" and demeaning language that all African American performers—musicians, actors, dancers, and others—were having to endure in media representations of their professions. Misconceptions about black prowess, based on such elements as temperament or physiology or "natural" talent, were so common that they continue to persist, if under the surface, to this day.

This, then, was the environment in which Owens and Louis came to prominence. The federal government had been segregated by the "great peacemaker" Woodrow Wilson. The US military was segregated. Services, transportation, housing, and schools were segregated. Voting rights and civic participation were denied on the basis of race. National politics were steered toward maintaining the status quo by southern Democrats. Most important, American culture was imbued with a segregationist mentality. And though many white individuals had progressive ideas about race, the institutions that shaped their everyday life remained driven by fundamental falsehoods.

So the essential contribution of these great athletes—and many others whose names are not as celebrated—was pride in their achievements: their own personal pride and the pride and confidence they instilled in the African American community. When Max Schmeling—mature, skillful, wily—broke the heart of black America in the 1936 fight with a staggering sequence of blows in the twelfth round, it simply set the stage for Louis's determined and disciplined application of his great gifts. At Blackburn's insistence, he returned to the ring within two months. He beat the "Cinderella Man," James Braddock, to become world heavyweight champion. Then, exactly two years after his loss to Schmeling, Louis exacted his revenge in Yankee Stadium, giving a six-year-old Dick Gregory and millions of other African Americans a memory they would carry with them for the rest of their lives.

Louis would defend his title twenty-five times. But like Joe DiMaggio and Ted Williams, he lost his best years to the army, enlisting when he was twenty-seven. He fought nearly a hundred exhibition matches for the armed forces and donated his portion of the purses he won to military organizations such as Army Relief. Although segregation rankled with him (African Americans risk their lives, he said, "but they can't sleep in the same barracks with the white guys or go to the same movies or hardly get in officer's training"), he remained a patriot. He quietly fought racism in the military using his status, contacts, and participation in the creation of educational films. And all the while, as he was donating huge sums to

JOE LOUIS'S TAXES

THE IRS PURSUIT of back taxes from Joe Louis does not appear to be racially motivated. The personal income tax in the United States was a new phenomenon when Louis was growing up, and in 1931, when he began his career, only 2 percent of Americans even had to pay income tax at all. But the Great Depression and Franklin Roosevelt's New Deal required the creation of an expanded tax base, and Louis was financially successful enough that by the forties, when the top marginal rate had grown to 90 percent, he owed the government a lot of money.

Louis was also very generous. He used his earnings to help family and friends and people in need, and during World War II, he donated a number of his purses to relief funds for the army and navy, without thinking of the tax impact. So even though he came out of retirement to earn more money, he found himself without the funds to pay those massive back taxes—a situation that would dog him for the rest of his life.

the defense of his country and subsisting on a private's salary of $21 a month, the Internal Revenue Service (IRS) was pursuing him for $217,000 in back taxes.

The tax issue would follow him for years to come. His early managers, Roxborough and Black, had not served him well when they handed his affairs over to the white manager Mike Jacobs. Jacobs, in a pattern that many black professionals suffered from during these years, engaged Louis on business terms that were, in retrospect, grossly unfair (Louis received less than 20 percent of the estimated $4.6 million he earned during his boxing career). And Jacobs handled all the matters concerning Louis with the IRS!

Though ineligible for interment in Arlington National Cemetery, Joe Louis came to rest there after his death in April 1981 when President Ronald Reagan waived burial requirements.

These issues forced Louis to continue boxing well past his prime. In his late thirties, he was badly beaten by Ezzard Charles and Rocky Marciano. Over time, he would battle mental health issues. Drugs took a toll as well. When Louis died in 1981, Ronald Reagan waived the eligibility rules for burial at Arlington National Cemetery, and he was buried there with full military honors. Max Schmeling was a pallbearer. Louis's contribution to black culture was remembered by many and continues to grow. As Motown founder Berry Gordy said, "When Joe won, it was phenomenal to be black, because he was a hero to all the people. His title win and the victory over Schmeling was a defining moment in black history."

Like Louis, Owens was by nature an apolitical man who believed that every man should be judged by his individual accomplishments. "I wanted no part of politics," he once wrote. "And I wasn't in Berlin to compete against any one athlete. The purpose of the Olympics, anyway, was to do your best. As I'd learned long ago from Charles Riley, the only victory that counts is the one over yourself."

But history and injustice are hard taskmasters, and Owens's attitude would change as he grew older. The accolades of his Berlin triumphs faded quickly once he was back in Jim Crow America, and he soon found himself barred from the ability to make a living. He resorted to menial jobs and even raced against horses for cash. He was stripped of his amateur status and lost out on lucrative sponsorship deals. "After I came home from the 1936 Olympics," he said, "it became increasingly apparent that everyone was going to slap me on the back, want to shake my hand or have me up to their suite. But nobody was going to offer me a job."

Although he fought hard to regain his amateur status, the USOC dismissed his attempts to work out an arrangement. He went through several years of attempting to restore his good standing; like Louis, he ran into problems with the government, fighting off tax evasion charges. But he retained his equanimity, slowly revived his reputation, and earned a good living in motivational speaking, international coaching, and public relations. Even greater recognition followed, culminating in his 1976 reception of the Presidential Medal of Freedom, the highest national civilian award.

Yet he remembered not just Hitler's snub, but Roosevelt's. And he had learned enough hard lessons about the reality of Jim Crow to write in his 1972 book *I Have Changed*, "I realized now that militancy in the best sense of the word was the only answer where the black man was concerned, that any black man who wasn't militant in 1970 was either blind or a coward."

Jesse Owens and Joe Louis were neither blind nor cowardly. They were clear-eyed and brave. They came to stardom at the start of the modern era, when brand-new forms of mass media and globalization were drawing unprecedented attention to politics, sports, and culture. Their exploits drew worldwide scrutiny. Yet they had to live and function in a powerfully racist society that was unwilling to discard a legacy of racism that had persisted since the first slaves were brought to North America. The United States still struggles with recognizing and addressing this legacy, but the way that Louis and Owens generated African American pride and handled the massive challenges of their time was a huge step in the slow process of righting those wrongs. Along with many other black athletes of the thirties—in baseball, athletics, boxing, basketball, football, and other sports—these men set the stage for the huge changes to come in postwar America, including the revolutionary triumph of Jackie Robinson.

2 WE SHALL OVERCOME
Jackie Robinson

N THEIR DISTINCTIVE WAYS, Jesse Owens and Joe Louis were leaders. Louis in particular, especially when he was in the army, learned how to use his interpersonal skills to bring about meaningful change, usually in direct reaction to racial injustice. But Jackie Robinson, by the weight of circumstance and the force of history, had to find within himself the qualities of a *national* leader. This development was not easy. As the Harvard historian Nancy Koehn tells us, the character of great leaders, from Frederick Douglass to Abraham Lincoln to Rachel Carson, is forged in crisis. Leaders are made, not born, and great leaders pass through fire. Robinson was burned by the same fires of bigotry that affected all African Americans of his generation, but he was also fated to assume a unique and defining role in a national crisis.

The United States emerged from World War II with a changed perspective on race. The regional prejudices that had shaped national attitudes and politics for generations were blown open by the economic and social realities of a postwar landscape. Millions of African American men and women had served their country in a segregated military. Millions of women and men had moved within the United States, spurred by the labor demands of the war industry. People of different races and backgrounds were thrown together like never before. Women and people of color had been asked to assume responsibilities that until then, they had not been allowed to perform. All this change happened in a swirl of patriotism stimulated by the stark miseries of wartime.

So in 1945, America woke to a new consciousness around its diversity. Those who understood the issues could see that diversity offered a path to national unity. The war effort proved that the old hierarchies were false and unjust. Furthermore, the country had come out of the war with the world's strongest economy. After the suffering and strictures of the Great Depression and world conflict, the opportunities seemed boundless, at least for white Americans. The result of all this upheaval was a greater awareness of race among all Americans—and a greater awareness among African Americans of injustice.

But being aware of a problem does not solve it, especially as so many white Americans continued to see diversity as a threat. Progress would be partial, gradual, and painful. Over the twenty-five years following the war, the familiar racial milestones that we all acknowledge, pursued in the face of hatred and violence, came about primarily because of the leadership, bravery, and tenacity of the women and men of the civil rights movement: the desegregation of the armed forces in 1948; the *Brown v. Board of Education* ruling by the US Supreme Court, which declared segregation in public schools unconstitutional, in 1954; the Voting Rights Act in 1965; and the Fair Housing Act, passed by Congress in 1968, just a week after the assassination of Martin Luther King, Jr. All these accomplishments were hard-earned and historic. Yet before any of them, Jackie Robinson trotted onto Ebbets Field on April 15, 1947, taking his position at first base and breaking baseball's color line.

Getting to that historic moment in Brooklyn took great courage and moral effort, by Robinson and by many other men and women, black and white. But for Robinson, breaking into the major leagues was only the beginning of his leadership in the cause of fighting racism. We are right to commemorate that great step; we are right to display number 42, Jackie Robinson's number, in stadiums; we are right to celebrate April 15 each year, when all major-league players, coaches, and managers on both teams, as well as umpires, wear number 42 on their uniforms. But Robinson's long leadership legacy was forward-looking. In 1947, he knew how far America still had to go, just as Colin Kaepernick, Serena Williams, LeBron James, and other contemporary black athletes know how much work we still have ahead of us today.

Born in 1919 in Cairo, Georgia, Robinson was only five years younger than Joe Louis. But that five years was historically crucial. Like the families of Jesse Owens and Louis, Robinson's mother, Mallie McGriff, a hardworking, courageous, religious woman, would leave the hardscrabble existence of the Deep South for a better life—in Pasadena, California, in her case. It may have been better than where she came from, but California nevertheless had a racist environment in common with the rest of the country, not just for African Americans, but for Mexican Americans, Chinese Americans, and of course Japanese Americans, who were rounded up in great numbers and imprisoned for the duration of World War II.

The youngest of Mallie's five children, Jackie was intelligent, perceptive, and combative. And he had much to combat. His father had left the family when Robinson was an infant. As a child, he was pelted with racial epithets and denied sporting opportunities because of segregation. His older brother (and father figure) Frank was killed in a car crash when Jackie was a teenager. So he did what many poor young men did: He joined a gang, and he spent a brief time in jail when the gang attacked an innocent man riding a bike. Yet with the help of mentoring by two older African American men from the neighborhood, Robinson left the gang and channeled his anger and competitiveness into education and sports. Later in life, he would say that another positive force at the time was remembering the advice that his grandmother, Edna Mae McGriff, gave to him in childhood: "You are the equal of any man, white or black. Never accept anything different."

The Robinson family was blessed with world-class athletic talent. Jackie's brother Mack, four years his senior, was a star athlete in college and winner of the silver medal in the 200-meter run, behind Jesse Owens, at the 1936 Olympics. Jackie worshiped Mack, but his brother found it difficult to move beyond the barriers of Jim Crow; he returned from Berlin without fanfare and was reduced to sweeping streets in Pasadena, still wearing his Olympic sweats because he couldn't afford new clothes.

Jackie showed even more athletic brilliance. In high school, junior college, and at the University of California, Los Angeles (UCLA), he excelled in *five* sports—he was a star in baseball, All-American in football, Pac-8 leading scorer in basketball,

This bust of Jackie Robinson, in his hometown of Pasadena, California, sits next to a similar statue of his brother Mack, a silver medalist in the 1936 Olympics.

National Collegiate Athletic Association (NCAA) champion in track and field, and a decent tennis player. But he also had something that Mack—and most people—lacked: a fire inside that pushed him not just to earn athletic success, but to reach a level of engagement reached only by life's highest achievers. In sports terms, that meant superstardom and consistent championship performance that would later be achieved by athletes like Venus Williams and Michael Jordan. But in life terms as well as historically, Jackie Robinson's fire and bravery enabled him to call out injustice in the most public arenas, even when it put him at clear personal risk.

At Pasadena Junior College, Robinson thrived, even when the coach surprised him by sending several new, aggressive white recruits from

Oklahoma onto the practice field in a preseason workout. Robinson kept his cool. But in January 1938, just days before his nineteenth birthday, he was arrested coming to the defense of a black friend who was being harassed by the police. He received a two-year suspended sentence, but the incident make it clear: Robinson would not back down in the face of racial bias. Motivated and mentored by a local minister, Karl Downs, Robinson tempered his combativeness with religion, pushing himself to be mindful of the need to always channel his anger into battling oppression.

Robinson would soon find an even larger platform for his education as a leader. In 1941, after his senior year at UCLA, he faced the same problem that his brother Mack had five years earlier. In spite of showing outstanding athletic prowess, he struggled to earn a living in a segregated post-Depression culture, where *half* the African American population was out of work. After a brief stint in Hawaii, where he worked in construction and played football with the semiprofessional, racially integrated Honolulu Bears, he and the rest of the United States had their lives utterly changed when the Japanese attacked Pearl Harbor. In 1942, he was drafted into the army and sent to a segregated unit in Fort Riley, Kansas.

"We are not makers of history," Dr. King famously said, "we are made by history." And as history would have it, Joe Louis was also stationed at Fort Riley, setting the stage for a passing of the torch from one great African American pioneer to another. Upon arrival at the unit, Robinson applied for Officers' Candidate School (OCS). Officially, African American officer candidates were allowed to train in integrated facilities; in reality, however, few were given access to the school. Robinson was rejected. Off the record, he was told that black people were excluded because they lacked leadership ability.

Robinson went to Louis, who, though not an officer himself, was adept at working behind the scenes to address discrimination. Louis arranged a meeting for Robinson and other black soldiers to argue their case before a representative of the US secretary of defense. Within a few days, several African American men, including Robinson, were enrolled in OCS, and the following year, Robinson was commissioned as a lieutenant.

Yet officer status did not shield Robinson from bigotry. In 1944, a civilian bus driver in Fort Hood, Texas, told him to move to the back of the bus. Following the examples of Louis and Sugar Ray Robinson, who had refused to follow Jim Crow rules at a bus depot in Alabama, Robinson stayed seated where he was. He was then subjected to a series of humiliating confrontations, including being called the worst of racial epithets by a private and "uppity" by a captain and military police (MP) commander. He was charged with, among other things, drunkenness (Robinson was a lifetime teetotaler), and court martialed for insubordination and willful disobedience. Following a public outcry, the court martial ended in exoneration, but Robinson had had enough and left the army in November 1944 with an honorable discharge. He later wrote of his acquittal, "It was a small victory, for I had learned that I was in two wars, one against the foreign enemy, the other against prejudice at home."

The pride and courage that embroiled Robinson in military controversy were the very qualities that helped him evolve into the leader who would break baseball's color line. The impact of that achievement would be immediate and significant. Of the 26,000 fans who attended Robinson's first game in Brooklyn in April 1947, 14,000 were black. Hank Aaron saw Robinson play with the Dodgers in 1948 in Aaron's hometown of Mobile, Alabama. He was amazed. "This man . . . changed my life," Aaron recalled. Decades later, Aaron himself would receive death threats as he grew close to breaking Babe Ruth's home-run record. "I'm a patient man and I've been through a lot," Aaron said. "But I couldn't have done what Jackie did."

Institutional racism is more entrenched and more difficult to overcome than casual, personal instances of bigotry. Baseball was no exception. Although there was no written rule that barred African Americans, it was *understood* to be the case. And unwritten rules are always harder to fight than what is clearly documented. By the forties, there were many white baseball players, coaches, and executives who were in favor of integrating the sport, but the weight and solidity of longstanding prejudice were never going to be easy to overturn. And the czar of baseball during this time of Jim Crow was determined to fight against history.

In 1920, professional baseball had been in crisis: the Black Sox Scandal, in which eight members of the Chicago White Sox were accused of intentionally losing the 1919 World Series, had shaken the foundations of the game. Team owners willingly ceded control of the sport to Kenesaw Mountain Landis, a federal judge with a reputation for toughness. The segregationist Landis ruled baseball with an iron hand as its commissioner from 1920 until his death in 1944. He succeeded at ridding baseball of gambling, but he did nothing but discourage anyone in the game who even hinted at breaking the color line.

Historians have mixed views on Landis's personal attitudes (there were times when he stood up for individual African Americans), but his record managing baseball's institutional position on integration is clear and speaks for itself. To give just two examples, the owner of the Cleveland Indians, Bill Veeck, and the famous Dodger manager Leo Durocher both proposed integration to Landis and were both threatened with expulsion.

Integration made sense not just on moral grounds, but also for overwhelming practical reasons. African Americans had been playing baseball professionally since the 1870s, and by the 1920s, the Negro leagues had reached a standard that equaled or exceeded that of the all-white major leagues. The Golden Age of African American baseball—the twenties and thirties—saw the glory years of many of baseball's greatest players ever: Josh Gibson, Satchel Paige, Cool Papa Bell, and Buck O'Neill, to name just a few. These men played under shaky contracts in tough conditions, appearing in hundreds of games a year, competing and traveling in a Jim Crow environment, far from the privileged world of white baseball—and yet their teams beat the best white teams regularly in exhibitions.

Negro league baseball differed in style. It was faster, with speed playing a more significant role both on defense and on the base paths, anticipating the modern game. As the country's national pastime—not only the most popular sport, but also an intrinsic part of the culture—baseball, and the nation, suffered for excluding such an inspired version of the game, such wonderful players, and such an integral part of the population. Even people who cared little about civil rights knew that the color line in baseball was in no one's interest.

The story of Robinson's breakthrough has been told many times. It was not a popular cause. The mainstream press and its leading sportswriters, such as Red Smith and Arthur Daley, did little or nothing to support integration (Lester Rodney at the left-leaning *Daily Worker* was the exception). They were happy to watch from the sidelines. But the African American press, including the *Pittsburgh Courier*, the *Chicago Defender*, and the *Baltimore Afro-American*, lobbied long and intensely for the change. A glimmer of possibility appeared after Landis's death, especially when the more sympathetic Happy Chandler became the new commissioner. But even before Chandler started the job, Branch Rickey, general manager of the Brooklyn Dodgers, had announced the signing of Robinson to a minor-league contract with its farm team, the Montreal Royals.

Rickey was an innovator. He invented baseball's farm system and would become a major force in the expansion of baseball in the sixties. But his most revolutionary act was enabling Robinson to fulfill his destiny. Rickey had cut his teeth in the South, as the manager of the St. Louis Cardinals. After moving to the Dodgers, who were experiencing a shortage of players because of the war, and witnessing the success of the Negro leagues in terms of both performance and attendance, Rickey was ready to put into motion his most important innovation.

Rickey's experience managing in the tough, racist city of St. Louis meant that he had no illusions about what Robinson would face as the first African American major leaguer. When the two men met in Brooklyn,

Rickey used a now-famous role-playing exercise to set Robinson's expectations. Describing future encounters with racist fans, teammates, and opposing players, he fired every conceivable racial epithet at Robinson, reminding him repeatedly that he would hear all this and more in the heat of competition, and would not—*could* not—be able to fight back. Robinson wavered but agreed. Though effective, it was an ugly exercise that we can now see for what it was: another example of how racism was endemic in the United States.

John Thorn, MLB's official historian, has written: "Baseball's finest moment was when Jackie Robinson first stepped on the field in 1947. . . . This was a transformative moment. No man faced a harder challenge. No man could have walked more valiantly and professionally. Jackie Robinson is my great hero as a baseball player and an American." This official statement of admiration is based on knowing how badly Robinson was treated that first year and how he conducted himself on and off the field.

Documenting a few of these awful incidents is painful, but necessary. Some Dodger players hinted they would sit out rather than play alongside Robinson. The manager, Leo Durocher, nipped that mutiny in the bud. Opposing teams, notably the Cardinals, threatened to strike if Robinson played, but National League president Ford Frick, supported by Chandler, said that he would suspend any striking teams or players. When the season began, Robinson was the target of physical and verbal abuse: Pitchers threw at his head and base runners viciously spiked him; opposing players regularly called him the foulest racial epithet from the dugout; he was subjected to every kind of hateful behavior that Rickey had used in the role play, and worse. And yet, in a display of leadership that was incredible in a young man, he did not retaliate. Like Mahatma Gandhi and Dr. King, he used passive resistance to disarm his opponents and undermine their violence. It was the only strategy for the time, and it was all the more remarkable because Robinson's natural instinct was to be aggressive.

Of course, he also disarmed his opponents—and won over all true baseball fans—by being one of the greatest players ever. For the next nine years, until his retirement after the 1956 season, he was often baseball's dominant force. In his first year, he led the league in stolen bases and was MLB Rookie of the Year. Two years later, he was the league's MVP, hitting .342, driving in 124 runs, and again leading the league in stolen bases. His speed and aggression gave him range on defense and power on the base paths. He stole home—a rarely seen play—nineteen times.

The game would grow with him. He had opened the door. In July 1947, Larry Doby broke the color line in the American League, signing with the Cleveland Indians. Other players started moving over from the Negro leagues: Roy Campanella and Don Newcombe joined Robinson in Brooklyn, and Satchel Paige joined Doby in Cleveland. The game had been transformed. America had begun to change. But transformation is like birth: just a beginning. It must be sustained. And the pace of change was uneven. The National League embraced integration more readily than the American League. And some teams were particularly slow to hire African American players. They would suffer over time.

In the late forties, the New York Yankees and the Boston Red Sox dominated the American League. Yet both were slow to integrate. In 1949, the Red Sox passed on the opportunity to sign the great Willie Mays. It would be another ten years before the Sox signed a black player; they were the last major-league team to integrate (two years after Robinson retired). The New York Yankees waited eight years after Robinson's breakthrough before breaking their own color line, and as late as 1964, they had only one black player on their roster. In the World Series that year, they would lose to the St. Louis Cardinals who—ironically, given their previous poor record on race—were led by African American Hall-of-Famers Bob Gibson and Lou Brock, as well as future National League president Bill White and Curt Flood, a gifted player who would successfully challenge baseball's reserve clause in the seventies. By then, the Cardinals not only had great black players—they had great black *leaders*, who altered the game of baseball, on and off the field.

As profound as Robinson's impact was as a player, he was arguably more influential after his retirement in early 1957. He did not hesitate to use what power he had to support the civil rights movement, then at one of its most crucial phases. Joining the board of the NAACP, he chaired the Fight for Freedom Fund, a campaign to raise money for the goal of ending segregation by January 1, 1963, the centennial anniversary of the Emancipation Proclamation. He supported other organizations pursuing justice for African Americans, including Dr. King's Southern Christian Leadership Conference (SCLC) and the Congress of Racial Equality. He was unafraid to march and participate in picket lines. He was, as you might expect, unafraid to speak his mind.

Politically independent, he sometimes supported conservative causes as well as liberal ones. As a player, he testified before the House Un-American Activities Committee in 1949, effectively helping to blacklist the great actor and singer Paul Robeson. He was also a supporter of Richard Nixon in the fifties, after the then–vice president had supported an independence movement in Ghana. A businessman, he believed in the importance of breaking color lines in the corporate world as well as in sports—he was the first black television analyst for MLB and the first black vice president of a major American corporation, Chock full o'Nuts.

Yet the cause of civil rights was what drove him most, and he was hugely moved, as many were, by his involvement in Dr. King's March on Washington for Jobs and Freedom (the Great March on Washington) in August 1963. King himself said that Robinson was "a legend and a symbol in his own time," who "challenged the dark skies of intolerance and frustration." When conservative Republicans attempted to block the 1964 Civil Rights Act, Robinson publicly berated them. Some Democrats had also opposed the bill, but up to that point, Robinson had supported

Republican candidates for president. In 1968, however, he withdrew his support for Nixon (which greatly pleased his daughter Sharon). Invited to a reception at the White House after Nixon won, he went along even though he was no longer a fan. Bob Gibson was also there, and he recalled making eye contact with Robinson during the affair and having an existential moment, as if they were saying to each other, "What are we doing here?" and began looking for the exit. But Gibson had the sense that Robinson never really felt comfortable anywhere.

Robinson also knew that too much emphasis on his own achievements might mask the work left to do. He was particularly frustrated by baseball's ongoing resistance to hiring black managers and front-office personnel. African Americans were helping ball clubs win pennants and world championships, but the power structure of the game remained resolutely white. "I'm going to be tremendously more pleased and more proud," he said when accepting an award during the 1972 World Series, "when I look at that third-base coaching line one day and see a black face managing in baseball." Nine days later, he suffered a massive heart attack and died at a young fifty-three years of age. His death came two years before Frank Robinson (no relation) became the first African American manager in MLB.

In the long decades since his death, there have been posthumous awards, statues, buildings, and streets named after him, movies about him, and the retirement of his number 42 in both UCLA and all of MLB. As important as these tributes are, we can imagine Robinson, if he were

Jackie Robinson and his son, David, attend the 1963 March on Washington for Jobs and Freedom.

still alive, shaking his head at how America still fails so often to acknowledge what his leadership conclusively demonstrated so long ago.

As Dr. King knew, history connects and shapes us all. Every American is connected to Jackie Robinson and is shaped in some way, small or large, by the place that history created for him and the way he chose to respond to the whirlwind of events around him. Because within the matrix of history, we all have freedom of will. When faced with the choices that our times and circumstances throw at us, each of us takes a path. We owe it to ourselves and to our culture to shape our own decisions in the context of the great leaders of the past. Everything is connected.

When Colin Kaepernick, Malcolm Jenkins, and other contemporary athletes follow Robinson's leadership example, especially when their choices buck the existing power structures and put their reputations and livelihoods at risk, it is important to place their actions in the context of history. But we must also make our own choice about following their leadership in the twenty-first century, and about actively supporting the ongoing struggle for justice.

In the words of the renowned academic and author Michael Eric Dyson, when Kaepernick "decided to kneel during the performance of the national anthem to pay homage to black victims of police brutality, closing the gulf between patriotic ideals and the reality of black suffering, he was, predictably, met with the same charges of most every black person—whether it was Frederick Douglass or Barack Obama, Sojourner Truth or Maxine Waters, Jack Johnson or Malcolm Jenkins—who dared speak out against injustice: that he is un-American, unpatriotic, disrespectful, and ungrateful."

Today's protestors know from Robinson's example that speaking out is actually American, respectful, and grateful. History tells us so. And Robinson did so himself when he said, "If I had to choose tomorrow between the baseball Hall of Fame and full citizenship for my people, I would choose full citizenship, time and again."

LESSONS IN LEADERSHIP
Bill Russell and Jim Brown

3

GREAT BATTLEFIELD GENERALS rarely make great presidents. Leadership in the trenches doesn't easily transfer to the demands of political life. And though many athletes excel at inspiring and directing their teammates, by word or example, game by game and season by season, few of them can negotiate the politically complex challenges of unfair work practices or institutional racism.

But greatness brings high expectations. To be among the best in the world requires huge talent, of course, but also a fierce work ethic, intense competitiveness, and immense self-belief. Moreover, the greatest must move outside the narrow focus of their ability and acknowledge that others will look to them for leadership. Will *expect* leadership—especially if issues of race, class, or gender add a political dimension. This was true of Frederick Douglass. Of Harriet Tubman and Thurgood Marshall. And of Bill Russell and Jim Brown, the greatest at their chosen professions of basketball and football, respectively, in their time, if not for all time.

Bill Russell shares a joke with Boston mayor Tom Menino at a 2013 ceremony at Boston City Hall honoring Russell.

They were almost exact contemporaries, both born in the Deep South in the heart of the Great Depression. And they had remarkably similar backgrounds. But Russell and Brown would handle the demands of leadership in very different ways. Their sports careers coincided with a period of vocal racism and often violent struggle as the civil rights movement fought to fulfill Dr. King's dream. The decade of 1955–1965 was a critical period for African Americans. It was also a time of rising notoriety for sports stars, when mass media turned professional sports—especially the NFL and the NBA—into a countrywide obsession. Russell and Brown were among America's most famous citizens, and yet they were also black men who knew from their own bitter experience that fame and money and prestige did not insulate them from bigotry.

They were also individuals, with their own unique temperaments and political beliefs. Unlike Jackie Robinson, whose entry onto the world stage was carefully planned and rigorously monitored, Russell and Brown rose to the peak of their professions with the assumption that the hard work of crossing the color line in professional sports had been completed. In 1950, Chuck Cooper, Nat Clifton, and Earl Lloyd had been the first African Americans to play in the NBA. The NFL (which had been fitfully integrated in the twenties before becoming fully segregated) had a series of signings of black players in the late forties, led by UCLA star Kenny Washington. By the mid-fifties, when Russell and Brown were drafted in the first round by the Boston Celtics and Cleveland Browns, respectively, integration in both leagues was at a kind of midpoint, and in this tense limbo of racial ambiguity, it's not surprising that these two great players would bear much of the weight of African American frustration at ongoing discrimination.

Once the color line in sports was broken, it was as if liberal white Americans exhaled in relief and said, "OK, that's done." It was tempting to assume that the hard work of integration was over and that progress would follow naturally. But history does not happen that way. Consider 1963, nine years after *Brown v. Board of Education* and sixteen years after Jackie Robinson's milestone: Russell, at the height of his powers as the NBA's most dominant player, led the Boston Celtics to their fifth consecutive title and their sixth in the seven seasons he had played with them. The world champion Los Angeles Dodgers featured an opening-day baseball lineup that was majority African American. And Brown, the best player in the NFL, rushed for 1,863 yards for the Cleveland Browns—an NFL record at the time and still a franchise record more than a half-century later.

On the surface, integration was a concrete achievement, at least in the world of professional sports. But beyond that narrow world, 1963 was a bad year for many African Americans. In January, Alabama governor-elect George Wallace pledged "segregation forever" in his inaugural speech, and by April, just days after Dr. King had begun his first nonviolent campaign in the South, police used dogs and cattle prods on demonstrators, as Birmingham police commissioner Bull Connor unleashed high-powered fire hoses on black schoolchildren. In June, King was arrested in Florida for trying to integrate restaurants, federal troops were called in to force Wallace to accept black students at the University of Alabama, and the KKK murdered NAACP leader Medgar Evers in front of his home in Jackson, Mississippi.

Faced with such terrorism, in August, King led the Great March on Washington, where a quarter of a million demonstrators (including Russell and Robinson) listened to his "I Have a Dream" speech in front of the Lincoln Memorial. But the violence continued, as Wallace remained intransigent and President John F. Kennedy had to federalize the Alabama National Guard to prevent Wallace from using it to stop public school desegregation. Then, on September 15, a horrible atrocity occurred: the KKK bombed the 16th Street Baptist Church in Birmingham, killing four young black girls as they prepared their Sunday school lesson on "the love that forgives."

These terrible events did not occur in a vacuum. They were the culmination of a poisonous reaction to the civil rights movement, which had been gaining in force and influence for a decade. And while the South was the scene of the most pathological reaction, racism remained a nationwide phenomenon. Even the experience of the nation's biggest sports stars bore witness to that. The events of 1963 began what would prove to be America's most violent decade of the century, marked by assassinations, riots, and the unpopular Vietnam War, and the violence showed, in large part, the tearing-apart of a country beset by problems of its own making.

Sports doesn't just reflect society, it interacts with it, and the African American athletes of this time practiced their professions in an atmosphere of tension and fear that affected them daily. And as the last generation to grow up in a prewar, Jim Crow environment, they did so without the advantages of an integrated upbringing.

Born in segregated rural Louisiana in 1934, Bill Russell moved with his family to Oakland, California, when he was eight years old. His mother died soon after, and his father worked hard to make a living and raise his children on his own in an impoverished neighborhood. A defining moment in Russell's life was being offered a basketball scholarship to the University of San Francisco (USF)—a chance, in his mind, to escape poverty and racism. Well, he would no longer be poor, but racism remained—on campus, on the road, and on the basketball court. After his junior year at USF, when he was Most Outstanding Player of the NCAA Men's Basketball Tournament and clearly the best player in the country, California journalists chose a white player over Russell as the best player in *northern California*. "At that time," Russell has said, "it was never acceptable that a black player was the best."

But he *was* the best, leading USF to two national championships and leading the US Olympic basketball team to a gold medal in Melbourne in 1956, before beginning his unparalleled career with the Celtics, the only professional team he played for. Russell revolutionized the game, directing Olympian physical talent with an outstanding basketball mind. "So many of today's sports psychologists," NBA executive Pete Babcock has said, "instruct players to use mental imagery, visualization techniques. Bill Russell did that seventy years ago. The reason he became a defensive genius is that he coordinated the techniques he had originated in his mind with his superior athleticism."

Russell believed that every time he played a game, he was the best player on the court. His powerful competitive spirit, superior intelligence, and transcendent skill set dictated this self-confidence, which, when communicated to observers, tended to spur one of two reactions: either admiration or outright resentment. He had many admirers, but the resentful stuck out. Touring with the NBA All-Stars in 1958, Russell and his black teammates were denied rooms in a segregated North Carolina hotel. In 1961, he and other Celtics players faced the same discrimination at a coffee shop in Lexington, Kentucky. About such incidents, Russell would write: "It stood out, a wall which understanding cannot penetrate. You are a Negro. You are less. It covered every area. A living, smarting, hurting, smelling, greasy substance which covered you. A morass to fight from."

But racism wasn't confined to the Jim Crow South. The morass was in Boston, too. "Boston itself was a flea market of racism," he would write in his book *Second Wind*. "It had all varieties, old and new, and in their most virulent form." Russell did not glad-hand fans or journalists, and his prickly demeanor outside the locker room rubbed many Bostonians the wrong way. Inevitably, it also provoked hatred. When he bought a house in a white neighborhood, bigots vandalized his home on multiple occasions. His outspokenness on civil rights irritated some in the press, who felt (as many journalists continue to feel) that sports and politics do not mix—as if sports take place in a fantasy world, apart from reality.

Many years later, NBA head coach Doc Rivers would comment: "Russell was all about the team, winning eleven championships. But he was willing to take a stand for what he believed was right, was just for African Americans. To do all of these things with all of the clear abuse that he and his family were enduring was just truly unbelievable."

Russell's pride and imperviousness to criticism had roots in his family background. When Quinn Buckner (also an Olympic, college, and NBA champion) met Russell and praised him for his courage and moral commitment, Russell smiled and told him that if Buckner thought he was good, he should have met his father. "My grandfather and my father," Russell said, "both used to say that every person had a line inside them that no one could cross. And that it was up to each person to learn about that line in themselves. No one could show them what it was, no one could make them defend it, but it was necessary to know that one could not live in peace with oneself if that line was crossed."

Russell liked to tell the story of how his grandfather, in turn-of-the-century Louisiana, built a schoolhouse for black children and faced down white supremacists who tried to stop him. This refusal to be intimidated, passed down through the generations, surfaced repeatedly in Russell, even when he was at the height of his fame. When Medgar Evers was murdered in June 1963, Russell was coming off of his sixth NBA championship. Hearing that Evers was dead, he flew to Mississippi at once. With Evers's brother Charlie, Russell spent the summer in Jackson building playgrounds and running the first integrated basketball camp in the city. The KKK hovered in the background, vulturelike, and Charlie often stood guard outside Russell's motel room, holding a rifle.

"It took tremendous bravery, commitment, and courage," Pete Babcock said. "And the Celtics deserve credit, too. Because when Russell took a stand like that, he was doing this as the face of the Celtics. Not only that, he was the game's best player. So he was doing what he did as the face of the NBA."

Jim Brown's background was notably similar to Russell's. He too, at the age of eight, moved with his family from his southern birthplace (in St. Simons, Georgia) and headed north (to Manhasset, New York). He too became a star athlete in college, excelling in football, basketball, the decathlon, and lacrosse at Syracuse University. And he too suffered the degradation of enforced segregation and white resentment. Although much has been written about the challenges of integration in southern colleges, many northern colleges, including Syracuse, also persisted in treating even their highly recruited African American athletes separately and unfairly.

At Syracuse, Brown had to live alone, in a secluded part of the campus apart from the rest of the football team. He had to battle the hostility of head coach Ben Schwartzwalder, who resisted adding Brown to the team, initially saying, "Not interested, he's colored." Schwartzwalder tried to sideline Brown on and off the field, subjecting him to segregation and humiliation, but by his senior year, Brown was a superstar who had elevated Syracuse to the national stage. Yet in spite of his obvious superiority

Jim Brown speaks outside the Webster Correctional Institute in Cheshire, Connecticut, after meeting with prisoners there in 2003.

as the country's finest college football player, he finished fifth in voting for the Heisman Trophy, college football's highest honor. As with Russell, the white men who assessed the ability of college athletes looked at Brown with racist blinders. They could not admit the obvious—that he was the best.

Brown made himself a promise when he left Syracuse: "For the rest of my life, I will never let anyone tell me what I can and cannot accomplish. As a black man in America, I would draw on that credo again and again."

When Brown arrived in the NFL in 1957, the league had a de facto quota system in place, limiting the number of black players (the Washington Redskins had no African Americans on its team, and would not until forced to do so by the federal government in 1962). This unwritten limitation was supported by a practice called *stacking*, whereby black players were made to compete against each other for a small number of positions. Acutely conscious of this unlevel playing field, Brown negotiated his early career with wariness. Already disenchanted by being benched at the college and NFL All-Star Games, Brown was the first NFL player to hire an agent. He stood up for black teammates and bridled at the jackboot style of Browns head coach Paul Brown, to the extent that he was branded a "locker-room lawyer" by team executives. He would become the first player to demand that a head coach be fired. Above all, he refused to be looked down on because of his race.

In athletic terms, Jim Brown's achievements, statistics, and durability, like Russell's, are astounding. In nine NFL seasons, he did not miss a single game—and he was the go-to guy for the Browns, carrying the ball on more than half of the team's offensive plays, so he had ample opportunity to get injured. He is the only NFL player to rush for more than 100 yards per game over an entire career . . . and then he walked away from football in his prime rather than continue to suffer the disrespect of management. As his biographer Dave Zirin put it, "He was the first black athlete to be bigger than the league itself."

But Brown's fame and influence did not end with his retirement from football. He would go on to become a movie star (including roles in the hit films *The Dirty Dozen* and *Ice Station Zebra*) and a defining cultural symbol, at a time when black masculinity and Black Power were potent forces in American culture. "Jim Brown is our Black Superman," rapper Chuck D has said.

For many, he defined black manhood. He had forceful and often unpopular views about how the challenges of African American identity should be met—views that remain controversial today. Uniquely, Brown found a balance as a player between self-respect and respect for authority—if you define authority in economic terms. His history as an activist is complicated by this balance, and further complicated by the fact that his notion of manhood had anger at its core—an anger that would lead to actions off the field that some activists would argue compromised his integrity and his legacy.

Russell and Brown were keenly aware of what Jackie Robinson, Joe Louis, and Jesse Owens had achieved, but they also knew that to be historically meaningful, this legacy had to progress to address the challenge of racism in a very different period. Russell recalled how Dodgers shortstop Pee Wee Reese had put his arm around Robinson's shoulders in Cincinnati as fans shouted racially abusive language, at the time a momentous symbolic gesture. "Jackie was my ultimate hero," Russell said. "He showed that we could walk with our heads up. But I would never have done that. I didn't need a protector. Jackie had already covered that ground for us." Brown put it this way: Robinson "had to play a role because of the plan

JIM BROWN AND THE LAW

JIM BROWN'S ANGER is a matter of record. In 1978, he was briefly jailed for beating up a male golf partner, and in 1999, he was arrested when his wife called 911 from a neighbor's house after Brown had smashed the windows of her car during an argument. He was also jailed after that incident when he refused to attend domestic-abuse counseling. A number of other incidents in which Brown was charged with crimes of violence resulted in the charges being dropped or the cases being dismissed. It is important to note that Brown himself has denied all allegations of domestic abuse—in fact, his refusal to go to counseling sessions (which resulted in the jail time) was because he did not accept that he was abusive, in that case or any other.

they had, and he made a vow to Branch Rickey to play that role. That was not his nature; if he did not have to do it for the betterment of the whole, he would not have done it. Joe Louis was a nice man that was kind of like that anyway, Jesse Owens was obviously that way. My attitude was, in no way was I going to be that way. . . . In no way did I ever feel that I would accept discrimination."

But the political evolution and influence of Russell and Brown would grow in very different directions as their athletic careers peaked and they became leaders and spokesmen for their racial community. At times, they appeared to come together in common cause: most famously at the so-called Ali Summit in 1967, when the two men, along with Kareem Abdul-Jabbar and other black athletes and civic leaders, met privately with Muhammad Ali for two and a half hours, questioning him about his religious beliefs and the champ's refusal to register for the military draft. That almost universally unpopular decision had cost Ali the heavyweight title and would result in his conviction, two weeks after this meeting, of draft evasion.

But the full story of the meeting reveals subtle differences in motive. Brown was the driving force behind the summit, and the participants gathered at the Cleveland offices of the Black Economic Union, a grassroots organization that Brown had established on the relatively conservative principles of black self-help and self-sufficiency. But Brown was also a partner in Main Bout, a company set up by boxing promoter Bob Arum and others, including members of the Nation of Islam, which controlled the closed-circuit television rights for Ali's fights. The US government had offered Ali a deal: if he would agree to perform boxing exhibitions for US troops, the government would drop the draft evasion charges. So Brown (and the Nation of Islam) had a clear economic motive for calling the meeting and trying to convince Ali to compromise his principles and accept the government's deal.

Ali, of course, did not back down. Quite the opposite—he convinced the group of the genuine nature of his protest. "We grilled him," Abdul-Jabbar said. "We wanted to be sure that he was sincere in his conviction." Russell was particularly impressed. "I envy Muhammad Ali," he said. "He has something I have never been able to attain and something very few people I know possess. He has an absolute and sincere faith."

Brown also spoke in praise of Ali, after the summit and many times to come, but as the sixties came to a close, his personal philosophy grew more individualistic. He endorsed Richard Nixon in the 1968 presidential election. He was disdainful of the Black Power salutes Tommie Smith and John Carlos used at the Mexico City Olympics that year to draw attention to US and global racism. He disparaged unions. And although he attended Dr. King's funeral, he was savagely critical of some aspects of the civil rights movement, saying, "I didn't like marching; I didn't march. I didn't like singing to get my freedom. And I damn sure didn't like singing 'We Shall Overcome.' To me that was weak."

Bill Russell understood something that Jim Brown, in spite of his greatness, failed to appreciate fully: that effective leadership looks beyond individual achievement to the needs and goals of the group—whether a sports team or an oppressed group of people. And sometimes it is necessary to suppress individual drives for the greater good. Russell's team focus on the basketball court was without peer, in any sport: in thirteen seasons in the NBA, he led the Boston Celtics to eleven championships, including two where he was a player-coach. Beyond basketball, Russell knew that the sting of racism was not just a question of pride (and he is a very proud man), but more important, a question of justice. And the pursuit of justice often requires standing up to the establishment, even when the establishment is convinced that it is doing nothing wrong.

"My citizenship is my birthright," Russell proclaimed. And he practiced citizenship as the pursuit of an ideal: justice and equality, not just before the law, but before all people. His vision of leadership was integrative. He was proud, and even arrogant when the occasion demanded it, but humble when humility was required. Humble in the face of Ali's religious belief. Humble in the presence of Dr. King's purpose and vision. When he attended the Great March on Washington in 1963, Russell met with King the night before the event. Join us on the platform, King said to him. Be there when I deliver my speech. But Russell said no. "I respectfully declined because the organizers had worked for years to get this together," Russell said, "and I hadn't done anything." But being there was doing something—he sat in the front row, and his presence, as the NBA's greatest player, was a powerful statement of support.

To be clear: Jim Brown was not afraid to stand up to the establishment, including the African American establishment. He was nothing if not an individual. And he often faced down discrimination with righteous rage. But here again, the question of leadership has made many activists take a closer look. Brown's belief in equality, it has been argued, was certainly as strong as Russell's, but as he grew older, he distanced himself more and more from many who shared the oppression of his own upbring-ing, especially black women. Intersectionality has never been his thing. Although the details may be disputed, the anger issues that mar his per-sonal history are a matter of record. The cult of manhood that has been a crucial part of his self-image—like the role of "gladiator" on the football field—can fetishize anger to the point that it becomes a false virtue. It is important not to dismiss the work he has done, including creating employ-ment and educational programs in marginalized communities and brok-ering peace between the Los Angeles gangs after the verdict in the Rodney King case in 1992. But some critics have asked: how can he square being a social activist with disparaging the civil rights movement?

Brown's response to the national anthem protests of Colin Kaeper-nick and others has been another example of his conservative, individu-alistic political view. At the beginning of the 2017 football season, he said, "I'm an American. I don't desecrate my flag and my national anthem. I'm not gonna do anything against the flag and national anthem. I'm going to work within those situations. But this is my country, and I'll work out the problems, but I'll do it in an intelligent manner."

When President Obama awarded Bill Russell the Presidential Medal of Freedom in 2015, the president was effusive in his praise of Russell's activism. It's hard to imagine him doing the same for Brown. There is, of course, a political divide here—Brown supported Donald Trump in 2016—and politics is based on shared values. Brown's values, as the years have passed, have remained fixed on attitudes that are not in tune with the expanding pursuit of racial justice as defined by activist organizations like Black Lives Matter, or the men of the NFL who choose to call attention to injustice by peacefully protesting during the national anthem in the tradition of Smith and Carlos.

Brown is entitled to his philosophy and his opinion, of course, but in addition to implying that the NFL protests are not intelligent, Brown's comment fits a pattern of resistance to the twenty-first-century civil

Bill Russell stands beside a statue in Boston's City Hall Plaza that honors his contribution to the city. One of the statue's granite bases is engraved with one of Russell's favorite sayings: *There are no other people's children in the United States. There are only next-generation Americans.*

rights movement that most African American observers believe is necessary. That pattern includes Brown's telling Trump that he ran "the greatest campaign in history." It includes taking offense at the words of civil-rights legend and US congressman John Lewis and calling the marches he led "parades." And it includes admitting that he "didn't think much of Dr. King. I mean, I am not trying to put him down, but if you think about the majority of the rhetoric, it's about what's being done to us. It doesn't have damn near anything that says what we're going to do for ourselves."

Brown's current stance does not cancel out his positive work in the past as a champion of African American rights, or the fact that he worked with gang members for decades and worked in poor neighborhoods helping residents build skills for success. But it does remind us that history is not static. And leadership—true leadership—shifts with history and accepts the demands upon it by all the oppressed.

In contrast to Brown, Russell's stance on the anthem protests has been unambiguously supportive. About the time that Brown was disparaging the movement, Russell tweeted a picture of himself kneeling (and wearing his Medal of Freedom), along with the message: "Proud to take a knee, and to stand tall against social injustice." He repeated the tweet a year later, at the beginning of the 2018 NFL season. Russell's tweet was the latest gesture in a long history of advocacy. This advocacy took many forms—not just the political, but personal and professional as well. He was a pallbearer at Jackie Robinson's funeral. He was a member of the 1964 Boston Celtics, the first NBA team to start five African Americans: Sam Jones, K. C. Jones, Willie Naulls, Tom Sanders, and Russell. When their teammate Tommy Heinsohn was asked about possible racial problems on the team, he dismissed this assumption forcefully: "We never thought anything about racial issues. We played the game. Color never was an issue with us."

By placing the team first and ignoring the barriers and prejudices that continued to mar sports and society, the Celtics showed that moral leadership makes a team better, not worse. And Russell (along with head coach Red Auerbach) stood proudly at the center of the bold and brave moves that resulted not just in great team success, but also social progress. "Star players," Russell would write later, "have an enormous responsibility beyond statistics—the responsibility to pick up their team and carry it." This belief, a core component of his success as an athlete and a coach, has remained Russell's credo throughout his life, and it continues to inspire those who support the ongoing hard work of creating an equal and just society.

4 THROWING THUNDER IN JAIL
Muhammad Ali

DURING PRESIDENT BARACK OBAMA'S time in office, the president kept two pieces of boxing memorabilia in the Oval Office: a pair of Muhammad Ali's gloves, signed by the champion, and a print of one of the most iconic photographs in sports history: the twenty-three-year-old Ali standing over Sonny Liston, sprawled across the canvas just after Ali knocked him out, less than two minutes into the first round of their second championship bout.

After Ali's death in 2016, Obama composed a warm tribute that referenced these mementos and included these words: "He stood with King and Mandela; stood up when it was hard; spoke out when others wouldn't. His fight outside the ring would cost him his title and his public standing. It would earn him enemies on the left and the right, make him reviled, and nearly send him to jail. But Ali stood his ground. And his victory helped us get used to the America we recognize today. Muhammad Ali was The Greatest. Period. If you just asked him, he'd tell you. He'd tell you he was the double greatest; that he'd 'handcuffed lightning, thrown thunder into jail.'"

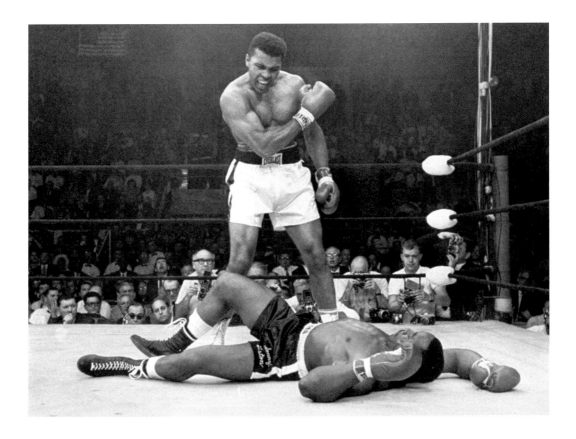

Since the opening ceremony of the 1996 Olympics in Atlanta, when Ali, just fifty-four years of age, shook visibly from Parkinson's disease as he lit the Olympic flame, he has been a generally beloved figure across the United States. But as Obama reminded us, it was not always that way. Like Dr. King and Nelson Mandela, he was considered to be the devil before he was a hero. His brashness and willingness to use harsh language about anyone—but mostly about his opponents in the ring—added fuel to the resentment fired up by his unpopular choices: to convert to Islam, a religion that most Americans consider suspect; to refuse to fight for his country; and to sacrifice his heavyweight title, the prime years of his talent, and untold millions of dollars (for himself and others) rather than submit

Muhammad Ali stands over Sonny Liston in the first round of their controversial second fight in Lewiston, Maine, in May 1965—one of the century's most iconic sports photos.

to the draft. It's a fact: he was hated. For who he was and what he stood for. In the glow of his celebrated status, it is easy to forget that historical reality.

"I am America," Ali once declared. "I am the part you won't recognize. But get used to me—black, confident, cocky; my name, not yours; my religion, not yours; my goals, my own. Get used to me."

America did get used to Ali—but only after the years of disruption and intense social combativeness had passed. Only when his physical gifts had been ravaged by a disease brought on by the sport he was so passionate about. As the NFL player and activist Michael Bennett recently reminded us, the power brokers of professional sports in America—almost exclusively white men—have always been opposed to African American athletes standing up for their rights and the rights of their community. Speaking of Colin Kaepernick, Bennett has said that NFL owners "are scared because his political views—that black people shouldn't be killed in the streets by police and should be empowered—are threatening to white society." He claimed that they were objecting to him being both an athlete and an activist. "It's like saying you can't be a father and a husband at the same time," Bennett said.

Many white Americans saw Muhammad Ali as the ultimate political threat. In 1967, when he was twenty-five years old and undisputedly the best boxer—if not the best athlete—in the world, Ali was so famous a figure and so powerfully divisive an activist that the establishment believed that it was necessary to destroy his career. In May of that year, he went to the US District Courthouse in Houston to face the consequences of his decision not to register for the draft and be sent to Vietnam. It was an entirely legal decision, driven by faith and integrity, but the authorities (and the nation at large) were intimidated enough to strip him of his title and send him to seek justice in the courts. He did not find it. Less than two months later, those courts would find him guilty, fine him, and sentence him to five years in jail.

In the short period between Ali's Houston appearance and his trial, Jim Brown organized the Ali Summit in Cleveland. Imagine the stress that Ali must have been under at the time. His most significant professional achievement, the heavyweight crown, had been taken from him. His ability to make a living was suddenly gone. His religious identity had been mocked and his racial identity vilified. And yet, in spite of these enormous pressures, he met willingly with many of his African American peers, knowing they had their own questions. They were aware of what he was giving up, financially and in every other way. They wondered what the real story was. And yet those men—Bill Russell, Jim Brown, Kareem Abdul-Jabbar, and other athletes, some of whom had served in the military and were not comfortable with his stand—came away from that meeting in awe of the champion's religious sincerity and rocklike integrity. There was no ulterior motive. Ali meant what he said and would face adversity calmly and resolutely, strengthened by his religion and his belief in himself.

Twenty-five years old. At the peak of his physical prowess. Young as he was, though, Ali knew what took most of America decades to appreciate: that what many saw as a foolish, immature, unpatriotic decision by a young man was in fact a critical point in a lifetime's spiritual journey, a journey that had led him to the Muslim faith and set the stage for a magnificent comeback that not only was athletically unparalleled, but also would give him immense credibility as an activist and leader.

Ali's background foreshadowed this remarkable journey. He was born Cassius Marcellus Clay Jr. (his "slave name," as he would call it in later years), in Louisville, Kentucky, in 1942. His parents were working people, Methodist and Baptist, and lived in a modest cottage in Louisville's West End. Given the time and place, the story of his upbringing is the familiar one of poverty, segregation, and humiliation. But he must have had enough charm and spunk from the beginning to impress community leaders, like the nun who gave him a job dusting in the library she ran, or Joe Martin, a policeman who ran a gym in his spare time and suggested to the twelve-year-old Ali that he take up boxing. His path to greatness was swift. Over the next five years, he would win six Kentucky Golden Gloves titles, two national Golden Gloves titles, and an AAU national title. His amateur career peaked at the 1960 Olympics in Rome, where he won the light heavyweight boxing gold medal at the age of eighteen.

By then, he was also keenly aware of everyday racism and his emerging religious destiny. Later, he would say that when he returned from Rome, and he and a friend were refused service at a restaurant because of their race, he threw his gold medal into the Ohio River in disgust. The story is disputed, but the sentiment is true: how galling must it have been to represent your country at the highest sporting level and then suffer such an indignity? But that was the norm for African Americans, even the most accomplished—it had happened to Jesse Owens, Jackie Robinson, Bill Russell, and millions of other, less famous black Americans throughout the period of Jim Crow.

Ali's father, Cassius Clay Sr., was unafraid to voice his anger and blame segregation and racism for the family's impoverishment. In Ali, that anger took a different turn. In a letter Ali wrote to his wife in 1964, he described how, while still a teenager in Louisville, he had noticed a man in a black mohair suit distributing newspapers for the Nation of Islam. He accepted a paper, and a cartoon caught his eye: a white slaveholder was beating his African American slave and insisting that he pray to Jesus. It occurred to him that, though he had been baptized a Baptist, he had not chosen Christianity. And though he had been named Cassius Clay, he had not chosen his name. Both were ultimately handed down to him by the white owners of his ancestors. Why should he respect either? "I liked that cartoon," Ali wrote. "It did something to me. And it made sense."

This was a remarkable discovery for a boy, and the basis for Ali's confidence and steadfastness later in life. It wasn't a question of reinventing himself; it went far deeper than that. It was about discovering his true identity via a spiritual quest. And that quest was driven by the realities of racism. Soon after returning from Rome, he was attending Nation of Islam meetings. In 1962, he met Malcolm X, still a Nation of Islam leader, who became his spiritual mentor. Leading up to his first fight with Sonny Liston—the fight that would put him on the biggest map, that would win him the title of heavyweight champion of the world—he privately changed his name. The promoter of the fight, which took place in Miami Beach in February 1964, had convinced Ali not to announce his name change until after the fight was over. But he had made his choice.

That first fight with Liston was an amazing event, later cited by *Sports Illustrated* as the fourth-greatest sporting moment of the twentieth century. It's hard to appreciate now how revolutionary Ali's victory was, how fearsome his opponent was. Ali was a seven-to-one underdog. Liston was ferocious, intense, and considered indestructible. Trainers who worked with Liston, George Foreman, and Mike Tyson have said that Liston was the hardest hitter among them. Harder than Foreman and Tyson! What was more, all the degradation and disrespect that had marked Liston's life as a poor boy growing up on a sharecropping plantation in Arkansas had stoked his anger and determination. His criminal record and ties to the Mafia added to his mystique. By comparison, the fresh-faced, twenty-two-year-old Ali appeared to conduct himself like an adolescent braggart, a callow youth.

But Ali backed up his brash talk with his fists, prevailing in that epic fight in seven rounds, dancing around the man whom he had taunted as the "big ugly bear," ducking, dodging, and ultimately overpowering the champion. To the amazement of journalists and fans, he took control of the fight. In the second round, he cut Liston, the first time any opponent had done so. In the fifth, he fought with a substance in his eyes that nearly blinded him (some theorize that Liston's corner had deliberately placed caustic material in a spot that would rub into Ali's eyes). In what would be the final round of fighting, the sixth, Ali landed overhand rights, lefts, and then three lightning-quick combinations. If Liston hadn't stayed on his stool and failed to come out for the next round, it was widely believed that Ali would have knocked him out. Victory gave the world its first glimpse of the "Ali Shuffle" and his glorious parade around the ring as he shouted the truest lines ever spoken by a boxer: "I am the greatest! I am the king of the world!"

Almost immediately, Ali's religious decisions became world news. Within days of the fight, he announced that he had joined the Nation of Islam and taken the name Cassius X. The following month, Nation of Islam leader Elijah Muhammad renamed him Muhammad Ali, which means "beloved of God." It was a very controversial move. The Nation of Islam was seen by almost everyone outside the organization as a divisive cult that unwisely and provocatively insisted on segregation. (And it is important to understand that the Nation of Islam was not, and is not, to be confused with traditional Sunni Islam.) Dr. King was explicit in his opposition. But Ali heard the message that his father had been giving him since childhood, though in a different voice. Elijah Muhammad promised deliverance from the evils of white civilization: dope, alcohol, adultery, thievery, and suppression. The Nation of Islam preached a spartan existence of prayers and fitness. It would provide Ali with a spiritual home.

It is important to understand that Ali's religious quest was evolutionary—a series of stepping stones to maturity and enlightenment. Much of what the Nation of Islam taught (or what Ali understood it to teach) was raw and undigested. The young Ali claimed to believe some outlandish concepts, including the existence of a space platform orbiting Earth, ready to drop bombs that would initiate an Armageddon as punishment for humanity's sins. He even claimed to have seen this platform. But the literal belief system was less the point at this stage of his religious progress than its symbolism. Ali was taking a stand, seeking a path that was active rather than passive.

The mid-sixties were years of enormous emotion around the present and future of African American activism. As the civil rights movement celebrated the legislative milestones of Lyndon Johnson's Great Society—primarily the Civil Rights Act of 1964—other militant groups were looking for alternatives to King's doctrine of non-violent protest. The Black Panthers, the Nation of Islam, and other organizations preached separatism and even violence. African Americans spoke in a multitude of voices, which often clashed with each other. And even within each movement, there could be bitter conflict—such as when Malcolm X broke with Elijah Muhammad and was assassinated less than a year later. Eventually, Ali (like many others who had been impatient for dramatic change) would see that Dr. King and his movement were anything but passive—but overall, this was an era of agitation and confusion.

In March 1967, Muhammad Ali and Dr. Martin Luther King Jr. tell reporters in Louisville, Kentucky, that the sooner the US does away with the military draft, the better off the country will be.

Like Malcolm, Ali would in time leave behind the extremism of the Nation of Islam and seek a more peaceful path in Sunni and then Sufi Islam. But in the sixties, the Black Muslim movement gave him the context for his pride in being African American and the strength of his opposition to racism and war. He had a global voice, and he was going to use it to draw attention to injustice and to seek change. As the writer and activist James Baldwin said in his book *The Fire Next Time*, Ali's search was for a movement that gave a broader definition of the black experience than Christianity had provided, that looked for an alternative.

The life decisions that Ali made public in 1964 would become inseparable from his fame and athletic talent. For the next three years, he would cut a swathe through the finest boxers in the world. The curve of his talent was upward: he was getting better and better, which made the stripping of his title and exile during his prime all the more tragic.

First, there was the rematch with Liston, in Lewiston, Maine, in February 1965, the fight where Liston went down to the infamous "phantom punch" in less than two minutes. Marred by controversy, death threats, and allegations that Liston took a dive, and forever memorialized by the famous photograph that President Obama kept in his office, this fight ended the dark spell of Liston and replaced it with the bright mystique of Muhammad Ali, a man who would do things his way, in and out of the ring, and would reign with charm, integrity, wit, and courage. Oh, and supreme talent.

But Ali's next title fight, against Floyd Patterson six months later in Las Vegas, presented an entirely different political challenge. Liston had been portrayed by the mostly white media as a boogeyman, a stereotypically threatening figure who haunted urban streets and allied himself with the criminal underground. Patterson was stereotyped in the opposite fashion. Although he had come up the hard way, battling racism and moving beyond his own criminal past, Patterson was presented by the media as a "nice Negro" who would put Ali in his place. To an extent, Patterson played the part. He was carefully inoffensive. He had been invited to the White House. The majority of fight fans rooted for him, and Frank Sinatra had written him letters of support. Along with Joe Louis, who said that Ali would "earn the public's hatred because of his connections with the Black Muslims," Patterson focused on Ali's religion. He wrote in *Sports Illustrated*, "Cassius Clay is disgracing himself and the Negro race.... Cassius Clay must be beaten and the Black Muslim scourge removed from boxing."

It was an unfortunate mixture of animosities between two African American men who had more in common than they thought. Ali used the public politicization to fire himself up. In the months leading up to the match, Patterson persisted in calling Ali "Clay." Ali countered by calling Patterson an "Uncle Tom." Later in life, Ali would say that of all the men he fought, Patterson was the most skilled as a boxer. But that night was no contest. Ali dominated from the start. And he was cruel. Instead of scoring a quick knockout, he drew the fight out, mocking and punishing Patterson until the referee stopped the fight in the twelfth round.

The mostly white media said that Ali had been vicious and vindictive, but the Black Panther leader Eldridge Cleaver called the fight with Patterson "a pivotal event" in the black revolution. The fight remains one of the crucial moments in the history of the African American struggle in the sixties. It pitted two very different versions of activism against each other, and both sides were appropriated and misrepresented by the white establishment. But struggle is an evolution; significantly, when Ali took his stand with the draft board less than eighteen months later, Patterson came to his defense, saying that Ali was "being made to pay too stiff a penalty for saying and doing what he thinks is right."

Over those eighteen months, Ali defended his title seven times. None of the fights was remotely competitive, with the exception of his 1966 clash with British brawler Henry Cooper. So when Ali was stripped of his title that May, he was undefeated in twenty-nine professional fights, nine of which he was reigning champion. He was supreme. And then he gave it all up for his beliefs.

But as Ali's belief system was evolving, so was America's. As the Vietnam War was slowly revealed for what it was—a huge moral and practical blunder by the most powerful country in the world—Ali became a hero to many young people who had never seen a boxing match in their lives. In this excessively violent decade, the antiwar movement took strength and inspiration from Ali's pacifism and selfless actions, expanding his leadership from statements on race and religion to ones of national self-examination and renewal. He became a hero to the counterculture.

Yet in the mainstream, he was mocked. *Sports Illustrated* said, "Without his gloves on, Ali is just another demagogue and an apologist for his so-called religion, and his views on Vietnam don't deserve rebuttal." The Federal Bureau of Investigation (FBI) monitored his movements and wiretapped his phone. Pennsylvania congressman Frank Clark claimed that Ali "turns my stomach." Many white sportswriters raged. Red Smith called him a draft dodger, and Milton Gross said that he had "reached the boundaries of fanaticism."

Yet the fairest way to assess Ali's stance is to listen to his own words from that time. Soon after he was stripped of the title, but before his trial and sentencing, he was in Louisville, where he and Dr. King met privately and held a joint press conference before Ali visited several local schools and churches. During one of those visits, he made the following impassioned statement:

> Why should they ask me to put on a uniform and go ten thousand miles from my home and drop bombs and bullets on brown people in Vietnam while so-called Negro people in Louisville are treated like dogs and denied simple human rights? No, I'm not going ten thousand miles from home to help murder and burn another poor nation simply to continue the domination of white slave masters of the darker people the world over. This is the day when such evils must come to an end. I have been warned that to take such a stand would cost me millions of dollars. But I have said it once and I will say it again: the real enemy of my people is here. I will not disgrace my religion, my people, or myself by becoming a tool to enslave those who are fighting for their own justice, freedom, and equality. . . . If I thought the war was going to bring freedom and equality to twenty-two million of my people, they wouldn't have to draft me, I'd join tomorrow. I have nothing to lose by standing up for my beliefs. So I'll go to jail, so what? We've been in jail for four hundred years.

There couldn't be a more eloquent expression of his beliefs. What's more, the range of his concern about injustice is remarkable: he was standing up not just for people who shared his race, but for oppressed people and races everywhere. And the terms that he referenced were the classic American ideals of justice, freedom, and equality. For those who had the humility to listen to him, he was delivering a textbook lesson in applying the principles of the US Constitution to the tangled realities of a nation in crisis.

In August 1970—more than three years later—Ali's long appeals process led to victory in federal court, which forced the New York State Boxing Commission to reinstate his license and allowed him to restart his career. In June the following year, the US Supreme Court overturned Ali's conviction by a unanimous decision, but by then, Ali had returned to the ring for three fights, including his first loss, to then-champion Joe Frazier at a sold-out Madison Square Garden in New York City.

His comeback fight, in Atlanta against Jerry Quarry, was a significant event for African Americans. Atlanta was a black city in a state stained by racism. The city's African American elite worked hard to get the fight licensed in the teeth of fierce opposition from the bigoted Georgia governor Lester Maddox, and the run-up to the match was ugly. There were racist taunts, death threats, gunshots fired outside Ali's training camp, and someone even sent Ali the severed head of a dog in the mail. But the fight was a triumph: Ali won easily, a TKO in the third round, before a 90 percent African American audience that included Coretta Scott King, Sidney Poitier, and Andrew Young. The champion was back.

So began the second era of the Ali legend: thirty-two fights over eleven years, including several that have entered boxing history and popular culture as unique, global events that touched the lives of millions, and sometimes billions of people:

- The loss to Ken Norton, who broke Ali's jaw;
- Ali's defeat of Norton five months later;

- Victory over George Foreman in Kinshasa, Zaire—the "Rumble in the Jungle," attended by cultural figures such as James Brown and Sammy Davis Jr., and memorialized in film by the Academy Award–winning documentary *When We Were Kings*;
- Ali's dramatic victory over Joe Frazier in their highly hyped rematch, the "Thrilla in Manila" in 1975, watched by a global television audience of over hundreds of millions of viewers.

Muhammad Ali regained the heavyweight championship in 1974 and would hold it for four years. He was still the greatest. But there would be sadness in this run of magnificence. He fought for much longer than he should have and ended his career with cringing losses to lesser men— Leon Spinks, Larry Holmes, Trevor Berbick. He was weeks away from his fortieth birthday when he finally retired, and the damage to his brain inflicted by the long, brutal history of his career would be evident to the entire world when he lit the Olympic torch in Atlanta.

As he grew older, Ali softened his political rhetoric and rejected the Nation of Islam, but he remained committed and active to the causes of peace and justice. He visited Bangladesh, Afghanistan, and the Sudan, as well as a Palestinian refugee camp in Lebanon. Alongside Stevie Wonder and Dick Gregory, he took part in the Longest Walk, a protest march in support of Native American rights. His focus became more humanitarian, and his actions were always made credible by the sacrifices he had made for his beliefs.

Remarkably, this man who had stirred up so much controversy in the most controversial of times became a unifying force. Many of the African American leaders who had criticized his unwavering support of the Nation of Islam would come to admire him and offer their solidarity: Jackie Robinson, Joe Louis, Floyd Patterson, the NAACP, even Dr. King himself before he was killed. And they did so because they came to realize that Ali was moving the fight to the next level. He did it in his own style, with some bumps along the way, but he knew instinctively what the world needed to hear about racism and injustice—even if saying so cost him nearly everything. The sociologist and activist Harry Edwards put it this way: "Ali is probably the single greatest athletic figure of this century in terms of the black community, largely because he turned around the image of the black athlete. . . . Because of the impact of sports on American society, there was a carryover of dignity and pride from Ali's efforts that accrued to all black Americans."

The transformation of Ali from outcast to leader moves across time. His exile in the late sixties ignited a wave of activism that rippled all over the world. It began with the National Conference on Black Power, held in Newark, New Jersey, in 1967, soon after Ali's trial, which pressed for an African American boycott of the 1968 Olympics in Mexico City unless Ali's title was reinstated. Black athletes across the country grew more politically aware, and many of them formed the Olympic Project for Human Rights (OPHR), an activist organization that would have a world-shattering influence in Mexico City the following summer. Ali was at the symbolic center of all this activity. As Harry Edwards said, Ali was "the warrior saint in the revolt of the black athlete in America." And such would it be for decades to come.

But Ali's leadership also moved *backward* in time—he learned (and the nation would learn) that the quest for justice is larger than any individual, and he was simply the latest in a line of athletes who were battling racism, each in his or her distinctive way. Progress is incremental, depending on many leaders building on the hard work of the past.

Ali's growing understanding of this evolution is best seen in his relationship with Joe Louis. Early in Ali's career, there was a lot of trash talk between them. They were both competitive men who knew that one or the other of them was the greatest of all time—though they would never have a chance to prove it definitively, one way or the other, in the ring. That competitiveness spilled over into their political disagreements. But as Louis aged and exhibited the physical impairments of a career that went on too long (as would happen to Ali), Ali changed his tune. He knew what Louis meant to the African American community of the thirties and forties, and he began to see how important that was. He knew that Louis's struggle was the struggle of the entire community, and that they were the right men for the very different times they lived in. He also grew to accept how similar they were.

In that spirit, he invited Louis to his training camp in the mid-seventies and offered him financial help. And when Louis died in 1981, Ali would brook no criticism of the Brown Bomber; he is said to have offered the ultimate accolade to his great predecessor, in humility: "I just give lip service to being the greatest. He *was* the greatest."

They were both the greatest. Both were part of our history. As the activist and civil rights leader Julian Bond put it so well, "Ali is part of every American's heritage. Every American should view him with pride and love."

OLYMPIC PRIDE AND PROTEST
Wilma Rudolph, Tommie Smith, and John Carlos

5

MUHAMMAD ALI SHOWED how an African American athlete could be both a powerful symbol of dignity and pride and an engaged activist. His influence was global and long-lasting, and it came from athletic performance *and* political engagement. He recognized his ability to reach people, and he knew how to use it. And a crucial tool in his reach and symbolism was television.

Television changed everything. It changed politics; it changed war; it changed sports. It was the dominant communications technology of the fifties and sixties, and its spread was rapid and complete. In 1948, there were 35,000 televisions in the United States. By 1960, there were 52 million—at least one TV set in 90 percent of American homes. Television had the reach and influence of radio or newsprint, but it also had *action*. Now visual history could be experienced live, whether it was the inauguration of a president, the body count in Vietnam, or an astronaut stepping onto the moon. And for sports, it was a game-changer. The drama, the quality, and the personalities of the best athletes in the world could now be experienced firsthand by literally anyone.

Technology explosions in communications—radio, TV, the Internet, social media—create massive opportunities for influence. Television changed the fundamental role of the athlete in American society, and 1960 was its watershed year. That was the year that the Olympic Games were first broadcast in the United States, and over the decade that followed, this sea change would have huge meaning for African Americans—starting with pride and ending in protest.

African American athletes had been steadily expanding their dominance in track and field since Jesse Owens's surge of excellence in 1936. National television brought that dominance to the whole country and allowed black viewers to celebrate their identity as their heroes demonstrated their talent to the entire world. At the 1960 Summer Olympics in Rome, African American men won gold in the 400-meter run, the 110-meter hurdles, and the long jump. Rafer Johnson took gold in the decathlon—the demanding ten-sport event that traditionally determines the "world's greatest athlete" (Johnson's place in history was twice-earned: he would go on to work for Robert Kennedy's 1968 presidential campaign, and he was the man—along with football star Rosey Grier—who subdued Kennedy's assassin, Sirhan Sirhan, immediately after the candidate was fatally shot).

But as great as the African American male athletes were, the real star of 1960 was Wilma Rudolph, the first American woman to win three gold medals in a single Olympics: the 100- and 200-meter individual events and the 4 × 100-meter relay. Rudolph had already been a force in international track and field. She was the youngest member of the 1956 US Olympic team in Melbourne, where she won a bronze medal, and just before Rome, she had set the world record in the 200-meter run—a record that would stand for eight years. But her success at the Rome games—bolstered by the power of television—vaulted her to international prominence, which

Rudolph used as an opportunity for leadership, actively and symbolically pursuing civil rights for a number of marginalized groups.

Rudolph's triumph and her subsequent leadership broadened the definition of racial discrimination. African American athlete activism had been, and would continue to be, a mostly male affair. But sixty years ago, Rudolph started a dialogue that is only now coming into full voice. She defined an activist battle that is still going on. She may not have used the word, but she was an intersectional hero. *Intersectionality* is the concept that different identities or systems of social categories, such as class, race, sexual orientation, disability, and gender, overlap and apply to an individual or group. Rudolph experienced all the disadvantages of growing up black in the United States in the forties—but she was also a woman in a time when the oppression of women was systematic and widespread. And as if that weren't enough, Rudolph also had to overcome a physical disability that would have challenged the most privileged of sufferers—never mind a poor black girl growing up in the Jim Crow South.

The daughter of a railway porter and a housemaid, Rudolph grew up in Clarksville, Tennessee, and as a child, she suffered from several illnesses, including pneumonia and scarlet fever. But the disease that most endangered her life was polio, which left her disabled throughout her childhood, forcing her to wear a foot brace and then an orthopedic shoe. Like all public services in the South, health care was segregated. Rudolph was fortunate to have heroic parents who believed in themselves and in her. When doctors told them that their daughter would never walk again, they ignored the prognosis. When the segregated hospitals of Clarksville refused to provide adequate treatment, they found a hospital for African Americans in Nashville, on the grounds of the all-black Fisk College, that would treat Wilma.

Nashville was fifty miles away, but Wilma and her parents were undaunted. For two years, twice a week, she and her mother rode in the back of a Greyhound bus to the hospital, and thanks to doctors there, and to the in-home treatment her mother supervised, she was able to abandon the orthopedic shoe when she was twelve. She could walk. Then she discovered that she could run. *Really* run. The miracle of her recovery was followed by an even more astounding achievement. Four years after she discarded her orthopedic shoe, she was representing, at the 1956 Olympics, a country that had denied her equal access to schooling, health care, public transportation, and a host of other human rights. And four years after that—in Rome—she didn't just participate—she dominated.

After Rudolph's magnificent performance in Rome, Italian journalists dubbed her *La Gazzella Nera*, "the Black Gazelle," and she was feted worldwide as the fastest woman on the planet. She toured Europe and returned to Clarksville a hero. The city wanted to give her a warm welcome, but the twenty-year-old was already savvy to the power of her talent and her worldwide recognition, and she insisted that the homecoming parade and gala banquet be integrated—the first fully integrated event in the history of the city.

This instinctive act of leadership was the beginning of a new commitment. In 1961, Rudolph won the Associated Press's Female Athlete of the Year award. The following year, she made the stunning announcement that she was retiring from track and field, at the tender age of twenty-two. But she was not retiring from life. She saw that her larger purpose was to educate, so she finished her degree in education at Tennessee State, which had been interrupted by her athletic activities, and began teaching, protesting, and campaigning against segregation, and encouraging and coaching female high school athletes. She spoke regularly at schools and universities about injustice and served on a federal outreach program that brought athletics into underserved neighborhoods. She translated the symbolism of her journey into helping others.

Rudolph's activism was powerful but understated, as suited her temperament and sense of purpose. It was a strong but quiet form of leadership, not unlike that of Joe Louis. As the sixties marched on, however, and the turmoil of Vietnam, multiple assassinations, and the terror against African American communities mounted, a different sort of African American protest took shape, inspired by, among other things, Muhammad Ali's courageous and very public battle with the white establishment. So it was no coincidence that by the end of that turbulent decade, black athletes were using the reach of television and their platform to call out racism to a global audience. Ali, Malcolm X, the Black Power movement, and activist organizations the world over were defining a new language of confrontation. More than ever, the practical politics of activism could be linked to this symbolic language, which was subversive *and* universal.

There are certain years that define an era, and 1968 was such a year, full of life-and-death drama and intense contradictions. It was a year of killing, at home and abroad, and a year of yearning for peace. A year of radical protest, and a year when Richard Nixon was elected president. A year of Black Power, and a year of white disdain. Ali's imposed fall from grace had created an ironclad alliance between national politics, race, and sports. That alliance would be deepened by the actions of many African American athletes, culminating in the most visible, most televised moment of sports protest ever, when Tommie Smith and John Carlos stood on the medals platform after the 200-meter Olympic run at the 1968 Mexico City Olympics and, as the national anthem played, bowed their heads and raised their black-gloved fists in a Black Power salute (or, as Smith preferred to call it, a "human rights salute"). Now *that* took courage.

A lot of thought and effort by a lot of people were behind that famous protest. Television and photography create durable icons. But people create movements, and the key driver of that Mexico City moment was a man who would become a major force in African American athlete activism for decades to come, and whose influence is still being felt today—Dr. Harry Edwards.

A product of a stark, impoverished upbringing in segregated East St. Louis, Illinois, Harry Edwards was a multitalented young man with a powerful body and an even more powerful mind. At six-six and 250 pounds, he was a force on the basketball court, the football field, and the track. A specialist in the discus, he earned a scholarship in the early sixties to San Jose State University, where the famous coach Bud Winter had established one of the best track-and-field programs in the country, nicknamed "Speed City." But Winter's militaristic style of coaching and the familiar barriers facing black college athletes at the time—inferior facilities and accommodation, and little respect and attention off the athletic field—offended Edwards and brought him into frequent conflict with the coach. But he used his intellect and his curiosity to broaden his agenda, discovering literary and political heroes who would help him build a bridge between sports and activism: W. E. B. Dubois, James Baldwin, and Langston Hughes, as well as the voices of Malcolm X and Dr. King. After graduation, Edwards made a difficult but critical decision:

He turned down an offer to play in the NFL and instead headed for Cornell on a Woodrow Wilson fellowship, where he earned his doctorate in sociology.

Returning to San Jose State in 1967 to teach sociology and work for racial justice, Edwards met Smith and Carlos, two of the latest recruits to Speed City. The three men shared similar backgrounds: Smith was the seventh of twelve children of a migrant worker from Texas, and Carlos grew up in poverty in Harlem. The stars of a historic moment were beginning to align. "The goal," Edwards said later in life, "was to change the total understanding that the role of sports played in the black community."

His first move toward that goal was spearheading a radical movement on the front lines. Inspired by Ali's legal battles, as well as the expanding awareness that racism was both a national and a global problem, Edwards founded the Olympic Project for Human Rights (OPHR), with the express purpose of using the 1968 Olympics as a platform for international, highly televised protest. After a meeting that included Kareem Abdul-Jabbar, Tommie Smith, and San Jose State sprinter Lee Evans, the OPHR urged a boycott of the Mexico City games unless the following demands were met:

- The restoration of Ali's heavyweight title;
- The removal of Avery Brundage as head of the IOC;
- The continued exclusion of the South African and Rhodesian teams from the Games;
- The hiring of two black coaches and two black administrators to the USOC.

The establishment ignored most of these demands. But a lesson that Edwards had learned early was that making a demand was a meaningful activist gesture in itself. The issues had been flagged, and questions raised. The connection between sports and society had been made clear. So when Brundage kept his job and Ali's quest to get his title back began its long, tortuous way through the courts, thoughtful people the world over began to sense that something was rotten at the core of the elite group of white men who controlled international sports.

Let's remind ourselves: Avery Brundage, president of the IOC in 1968, was the same Avery Brundage who had headed the USOC in 1936. The same Avery Brundage who opposed the US boycott of the Berlin Olympics and given in to the Nazis when they demanded the removal of two Jewish sprinters from the 4 × 100 relay team. Now, thirty-two years later, Brundage was passionately defending two other racist, fascist regimes—the white-minority governments of South Africa and Rhodesia. International pressure had resulted in South Africa being banned from the Olympics in 1964. In 1968, Brundage and the IOC invited the South African team back, but the threatened boycott, from the OPHR and others, forced him to withdraw the invitation. Brundage also supported Rhodesian participation at Mexico City but was overruled by other members of the IOC.

As the Games neared, the difficulty of a specific boycott by African American athletes proved apparent. Most black competitors saw the Olympics as the opportunity of a lifetime, which they were reluctant to eschew. So Edwards and the OPHR turned to a strategy of individual choice. The athletes would make their own decisions about protest and participation. Some, like the long jumper Bob Beamon, who would make history at Mexico City by breaking the world long jump record by nearly two feet, made strong local statements. Beamon refused to compete with his college team, the University of Texas at El Paso, in a meet against Brigham Young University because of the Book of Mormon's teaching that blacks were damned by the biblical curse of Ham. Others, like Kareem Abdul-Jabbar, the best amateur basketball player in the country, who was still known at the time by his birth name, Lew Alcindor, chose to boycott the Games. Instead, he spent his time studying in preparation for his conversion to Sunni Islam. Finally, there were those, like Smith and Carlos, influenced by the OPHR agenda and inspired by

Edwards, who made the brave decision to attend the Games and subvert the event from within.

In the words of the NFL star and activist Malcolm Jenkins (who has the Mexico City photo of Smith and Carlos hanging in his home), "We as athletes now stand on the backs of not only John Carlos and Tommie Smith, but all the athletes who've risked their careers to speak up for the things that were not just or not fair in our country." The key word in Jenkins's quote is *risked*. Smith and Carlos knew what they were getting into. With Brundage at the helm, the establishment response was always going to be severe. Brundage himself had become a symbol of repression—and for good reason. He had made himself a target by clearly stating his sympathy with white-minority governments that were savagely repressing their black citizens. Racism wasn't just an American problem—it was a global problem, and the Olympics was a global organization. In response, the protest of Smith and Carlos was planned. But it was also spontaneous, in a way. The day before his 200-meter victory, Smith had told the press, "I don't want Brundage presenting me any medals." That night, he knew he would act on that statement of purpose, but he didn't quite know in what form.

Activists demand an investigation of the US Olympic Committee at a 1968 Washington news conference: (left to right) H. Rap Brown, John Carlos, Harry Edwards, and Stokely Carmichael.

The race itself, overshadowed by what followed, was electric. Smith and Carlos had drawn lanes three and four, considered the best for that distance. Usually Smith's style was to win with a distinct finishing kick, but this time he got off to a good start, though still trailing Carlos. Then he took it to another gear, passed Carlos at eighty meters, and pulled away in the final ten meters, winning in a world-record time of 19.83 seconds. He threw his arms in the air triumphantly, as behind him, the Australian runner Peter Norman moved ahead of Carlos for second place and the silver medal.

Then came the podium drama. Smith recalled it years later: "I had the gloves because I knew I was going to use the gloves, but I didn't know in what fashion. And that's when John and I talked about the idea of a victory stand. Everything was representative. Shoes, the idea of poverty; the black socks are, of course, power in blackness; the glove represented sacrifice and strength; the wreath in the left hand, the idea of peace, as an olive branch."

As expressed by the IOC today, the goal of the Olympic movement is to "contribute to building a peaceful and better world by educating youth through sport practiced without discrimination of any kind and in the Olympic spirit, which requires mutual understanding with a spirit of friendship, solidarity, and fair play." *Without discrimination.* Smith and Carlos were pursuing this lofty goal unambiguously and in good faith, and many throughout the world understood this immediately. In fact, Norman, a very religious man who took the silver medal in that race, wore an OPHR badge on the podium in support of the protesting Americans. Norman had known about the protest ahead of the run. It was he who suggested that Carlos wear Smith's left-handed glove (Carlos had left his black gloves in the Olympic Village). Norman would be vilified within his own country for this action, but ever after the men who had competed with him remembered his support.

PETER NORMAN'S RETURN HOME

WHEN SILVER MEDALIST Peter Norman returned to Australia after the 1968 Olympics, his 200-meter time of 20.06 seconds was an Australian record—and remains so to this day. He should have been a national hero. But he returned a pariah, marginalized by the Australian Olympic Committee for his conscientious support of Smith and Carlos. He would find himself excluded from Australia's Olympic team for the 1972 Games in Munich despite running qualifying times, and later, according to his nephew, Matthew Norman, he was not offered a role in the 2000 Olympic Games in Sydney "in any capacity." Upon his death in 2006, Smith and Carlos were pallbearers at his funeral. In 2012, the Australian House of Representatives made a belated gesture of restitution by passing a formal apology that recognized his great athletic achievement, commended his bravery on the podium, and acknowledged the "powerful role [he] played in furthering racial equality."

Smith and Carlos received plenty of vilification themselves. As we have seen, the media reaction in the United States was savage. *Time* magazine said that the runners had "turned the high drama of the games into theater of the absurd." Earlier in this book, we read Brent Musburger's nasty opinion in the *Chicago American*. The other black athletes at Mexico City had a mixed response. Two days after the 200-meter final, African Americans—Lee Evans, Larry James, and Ron Freeman—won all three medals in the 400-meter run. They wore Black Panther–style black berets on the podium but removed them before the anthem. On the other hand, George Foreman, who took the heavyweight boxing gold, waved an

American flag in the ring and invited Brundage to a victory celebration. As befit the tumultuous year of 1968, opinions were fiercely held and fiercely argued over, which made the Smith-Carlos gesture all the more courageous.

There was no question that Smith and Carlos were to be punished. But how? At first, the USOC simply reprimanded the two runners. But Brundage was incensed. After the race, he said that "warped mentalities and cracked personalities seem to be everywhere and impossible to eliminate," and he called the protest a "nasty demonstration against the American flag by negroes." So his attitude was clear. Via the IOC, he pressured the USOC to take more dramatic and punitive action. Two days after the race, Smith and Carlos were suspended from the team and expelled from the Olympic Village. At the time, several observers reminded Brundage that he had not objected to Nazi Party salutes at the Berlin Olympics. In an ugly display of hypocrisy, Brundage called the Nazi *sieg heil* an acceptable "national salute," while Smith and Carlos's gesture of peace and power was not national, and therefore unacceptable.

The OPHR project has passed into history—which means that, like all history, it informs the present as it illuminates the past. We see Brundage's agenda clearly. We see the continuity from Nazi sympathy to support for apartheid to racist decision-making—a pattern of thought and behavior that would be reinforced at the 1972 Munich Olympics, Brundage's last as head of the IOC. Harry Edwards, on the other hand, would go on to become a direct link from the radical sixties to the very different challenges of fighting racial injustice in the twenty-first-century. In the eighties, he became a special assistant to the commissioner of baseball, with the goal of increasing the number of people of color hired in the major leagues. He also consulted with the San Francisco 49ers of the NFL and the Golden State Warriors of the NBA on issues related to race and sports. Is it a coincidence that Colin Kaepernick played for the 49ers when he started taking his historic knee, or that the Warriors are now among the most racially sensitive teams in professional sports? Unlikely. Edwards, and history, connect Jesse Owens to Smith and Carlos to Kaepernick.

But the lessons of history are nuanced. They clarify past actions and present realities in many ways. They make us understand the *evolution* of activism. Jesse Owens's 1936 performance was clearly in the mind of the 1968 protestors. But as young, fiery men under the influence of radical politics, they didn't appreciate the complexity of Owens's achievement. They would protest where Owens had acquiesced. As if to reinforce this dichotomy, in Mexico City, the USOC recruited Owens to address the protesting athletes, including Smith, Carlos, and members of the gold medal–winning US basketball team. He spoke to them about the tradition of the ceremony, as well as what he had endured. He told them that "the black fist is a meaningless symbol. When you open it, you have nothing but fingers—weak, empty fingers. The only time the black fist has significance is when there's money inside. There's where the power lies."

Charles Scott was one of the basketball players at that meeting. "We looked at [Owens] as if he were completely out of touch," he would say much later. "We practically threw him out." As we have seen, Owens would revise his opinion about sixties militancy and accept that it was legitimate (and let's not forget—Owens had supported the boycott of the 1936 Berlin Games that was narrowly rejected by the USOC). But the young men of 1968 would revise *their* views as well. In 1979, Tommie Smith reached out to Owens with a letter of peace. And Scott has said that his rejection of Owens at the time was "probably the biggest regret of my entire career in athletics. We had *no idea* what Jesse had done. Being young, we made a huge mistake."

Smith and Carlos would go on to face life struggles partly created by their protest. The two had never been close, and there was some occasional backbiting between them, in spite of the way that history had brought them together. Both had brief careers in professional football, but the negativity surrounding their stand at the Games made it hard for them to earn a living. There were tough times for both men. Smith finally won acceptance in the late nineties, hired as the track coach at Santa Monica College. Both men were awarded an Arthur Ashe Courage Award in 2008, forty years after their protest. They have had statues erected and won presidential honors, but recognition was a long time coming.

Both have remained committed to fighting racism. Smith returned to San Jose State to finish his bachelor of arts degree in social science, and went on to earn a master's in social change and, like Edwards, teach sociology. Recently, he reiterated the positive spirit of the Mexico City protest. It was not about denigrating the flag, he said, it was about "human rights. Human rights came before the flag." Carlos has grown into a powerful speaker on behalf of human rights globally, with a knack for relating his personal history in a way that is eloquent, humorous, and politically sharp. Speaking of the Mexico City moment, Carlos has said, "All impact is eternal, and yet people couldn't understand that, then. People want to know because of all the recurring injustice and problems: 'what do you think you accomplished?' Obviously I accomplished something, because you're still asking about it."

Carlos is right. In the time of Colin Kaepernick, we are all still asking about the contributions of the activists of the past. Because African American athletes continue to constitute what Harry Edwards calls "the gladiatorial class." They continue to be viewed as mere entertainers who should keep their mouths shut about politics. But thanks to the sacrifice and daring of these courageous athletes of the sixties, we can have that wider conversation. Sports is no longer seen as only spectacle. These men and women demonstrated that there was, and always had been, racism in sports. They showed that the problems of the larger culture are recapitulated in sports. And they set a bar that a few brave athletes of today continue to strive for.

REACHING FOR THE SKY
Kareem Abdul-Jabbar

6

KAREEM ABDUL-JABBAR. The name itself has weight. Substance. It could be the name of a president or a prophet. But as we all know, it is the name of a man who has been a dominant force in sports, education, activism, politics, and culture for over fifty years. The name of a man who scored more points (38,387) and received more MVP awards (six) than any other player in NBA history, who has written fourteen books, who is known for his philanthropy, his love of jazz, and his commitment to religious freedom and social justice. As Barack Obama said when awarding Abdul-Jabbar the Presidential Medal of Freedom, the nation's highest civilian honor, "Physically, intellectually, spiritually, Kareem is one of a kind, an American who illuminates both our most basic freedoms and our highest aspirations."

The accolades are well earned, especially as they did not come easy. Abdul-Jabbar has met with resistance over and over because of the scale of his talent and the depth of his beliefs. He emerged to basketball greatness in the social cauldron of the sixties, when, as we have already discussed, African American athletes were responding to discrimination in a variety of ways. Abdul-Jabbar's response was manifold. Like Muhammad Ali, he changed his religion (though to Sunni Islam, not the Nation of Islam) and he changed his name. As Obama said, "He stood up for his Muslim faith when it wasn't easy and it wasn't popular." Unlike most, he used the power of the boycott in 1968 and refused to attend the Mexico City Olympics. He participated in the Ali Summit at only twenty years of age. And like Bill Russell, he used his leadership and talent on the basketball court to give African Americans a sense of pride and power, as well as to redefine how the game was played in the modern era.

Abdul-Jabbar is also a key figure in the history of college athletics, which for African Americans poses unique challenges that are an important part of the nation's ongoing conversation about race. Because he was so famous at such a young age, he had notoriety and influence long before he became a pro. As a prodigy at Power Memorial Academy in New York City, Lew Alcindor (as Abdul-Jabbar was known before adopting his Muslim name in 1970) led his team to a national championship and was good enough to be brought to Boston to be introduced to Bill Russell (Russell, in his typically brusque fashion, brushed the kid off; it would be a few years before the two men formed a close friendship). Fiercely recruited, he chose to attend UCLA, where the legendary coach John Wooden was forging the most dominant dynasty in the history of college basketball. He led UCLA to three consecutive NCAA championships from 1967 through 1969. As a player, he had everything: length, skill, athleticism, and a virtually unstoppable shot, the skyhook.

The fact that the skyhook was unstoppable was a notable irony—historically and (perhaps) racially. Abdul-Jabbar perfected this shot after the men who ran college basketball at the time banned the dunk. Today, it's impossible to imagine college basketball *without* dunking, but Abdul-Jabbar was so dominant that this rule change was crafted in a desperate attempt to limit his influence. And yet it actually expanded his domi-

Kareem Abdul-Jabbar shoots his unstoppable "skyhook" over Boston Celtics center Robert Parish.

nance, as he refined the skyhook to make up for the ban. Not Wilt Chamberlain, not Bill Walton, not even the seven-foot-six Manute Bol could stop the shot.

But Abdul-Jabbar's off-court legacy was also part of his character from the beginning. The young Lew Alcindor was religious, thoughtful, and engaged. His conversion to Islam at age twenty-one was quite different from Ali's instinctive conversion. For Abdul-Jabbar, becoming a Muslim was the logical culmination of a long personal process that integrated the words of the Koran with the teaching of African American leaders such as Malcolm X and Dr. King. As a high school student, Alcindor was hired by the Harlem Youth Action Project, which gave him the opportunity to interview King as part of a summer mentoring program. Tremendously impressed, he drove himself to understand how King proactively put into action the teachings of Mohandas (Mahatma) Gandhi. At that point, Alcindor, who was born into a Catholic family, was moving away from Catholicism, his belief in which, as he put it, was "always shaky." He was certainly aware that King and many other civil rights leaders were committed Christians (as was his college coach and mentor, Wooden), but as he pointed out many years later, "There were so many evil followers. White people who were bombing churches and killing little girls. The Ku Klux Klan were also proud Christians."

During his career as an activist, Abdul-Jabbar would utilize the teachings of Dr. King as a way of applying nonviolence to action within the existing political system. In 2015, he wrote in *Time* magazine that, rather than using the commemoration of Martin Luther King Day as a way of celebrating the end of racism, we should use the day as a moment to understand how the roots of the disease of racism still affect everyday life, if now more covertly. Voter ID laws, for example, advocated hard (mainly) by Republicans in recent years, can be used as a tool to discriminate against minorities, along with gerrymandering and police harassment. Yet Abdul-Jabbar also argues that we should never forget the important role that white people have played in the civil rights movement.

The most competitive of athletes, Abdul-Jabbar has always included the peaceful pursuit of change in his activism, which is consistent with the high ideals of his adopted faith. That isn't to say that pursuing nonviolence in the face of injustice is easy. As he has written, "Dr. King stuck to his convictions in the face of jail, in the face of doubt from within his own organization, in the face of ridicule from other African Americans. And the wisdom of his leadership has been proven by the success of the civil rights movement."

Abdul-Jabbar's status as the greatest college basketball player in the country—and his sophisticated political awareness—earned him a seat at the Ali Summit in 1967 and the privilege of hearing firsthand from Ali why the great boxer would rather go to jail and be stripped of his heavyweight title rather than go to Vietnam. "Being at that summit," Abdul-Jabbar has said, "and hearing Ali's articulate defense of his moral beliefs and his willingness to suffer for them, reinvigorated my commitment to become even more politically involved. That feeling of wanting to be part of a movement to ensure opportunities for all Americans hasn't left me since."

Ali's inspiration came at an important moment. In the summer of 1964, just three years before that summit, the seventeen-year-old Alcindor was riding the subway home from practice when he decided to stop off in Harlem. This iconic African American neighborhood had become significant to the sensitive and intellectually curious young man. A black cultural mecca, it had been the birthplace of the Harlem Renaissance, a reimagining of the black experience via the arts. It was the home of the best music in America. As a youth, Abdul-Jabbar was steeped in black culture. He had inherited a love of jazz from his father, an aspiring musician who was friends with some of the greatest musicians of the time, including Sarah Vaughan and Art Blakey. So he found Harlem a safe haven and a place of inspiration. But on this July day, as he emerged from underground, he found chaos.

Provoked by repeated police harassment and the police shooting of a black junior high school student, Harlem had exploded into a riot that would last six consecutive nights and destroy many local businesses and much of the area's spirit. And Abdul-Jabbar had walked right into the middle of it. "It was chaos," he said. "Wild and insane. And I just stood there trembling. Cops were swinging nightsticks at everybody, bullets were flying, windows were being smashed, people were stealing and looting. It was a scene I'll never forget. All I could think was that I wanted to stay alive, so I took off running and didn't stop for fifteen New York City blocks. . . . I sat there huffing and puffing, absorbing what I'd seen, and I knew it was rage, black rage. The poor people of Harlem felt that it was better to get hit with a nightstick than to keep on taking the white man's insults forever."

It was a defining experience. Years later, he would tell fellow basketball star Bill Walton, "I began to understand the need for activism that day . . . what happens when people react when they feel they are powerless." He realized that racism made him ill, emotionally and spiritually. He began to look for intellectual leadership and found it in the teachings of

Malcolm X. "Malcolm X was different," Abdul-Jabbar remembered. "His trip to Mecca made him realize that Islam . . . embraced people of all colors. His death in 1965 hit me hard because I knew he was talking about black pride, about self-help and lifting ourselves up. I read Malcolm's autobiography when I was nineteen, and it turned me around totally."

Abdul-Jabbar's balancing of an athletic and an intellectual life was fed not just by his reading and thinking, but by the history of the decade that he crowned so gloriously at UCLA. He was conscious of his place in that history. We are now so used to the dominance of African American athletes in college basketball and football, well beyond their proportion of the general population, that it is easy to forget that the sixties was the time when black athletes really began to make their mark in college sports, rising above the barriers that had been in place for so long. Abdul-Jabbar was building on the achievements of many black college basketball players who had come immediately before him: Oscar Robertson, Charles Scott, and Walt Frazier, among others. Abdul-Jabbar would play with or against all these men in the NBA, and collectively, they form one of the most powerful generations in the history of the sport.

Each of these players, like so many others, has stories to tell. Robertson grew up in segregated Indianapolis, and in 1955, he led his high school team, the all-black Crispus Attucks, to the Indiana state championship. In Indiana, there is no higher honor, and the championship game was televised statewide. But what happened after they won still hurts him. "The tradition was that the winner of the tournament has the parade through the city, where they're celebrated by everyone," Robertson recalled. "But for us, it was different. They forced us to have the traditional victory parade in our own neighborhood. To do that to kids, to embarrass and hurt them like that. Well, that's unforgivable."

Frazier would come to idolize Robertson and assume his mantle as the NBA's premier point guard, as he led the New York Knicks to two NBA championships. But as a poor boy growing up in Georgia, he hadn't even heard of Robertson. Where he lived, basketball games on TV were an all-white affair. "We were in the South," Frazier has said, "the racist South. They didn't televise basketball games with blacks playing. Just the SEC."

In the fifties, the Southeastern Conference (SEC) and the Atlantic Coast Conference (ACC), both representing teams in the South, were the homes for some of the best basketball teams in the country, including Adolph Rupp's Kentucky Wildcats and Frank McGuire's North Carolina Tar Heels. But these conferences remained all-white until well into the sixties. Charles Scott changed that when he became the first black player in the ACC. Originally from Harlem, but playing out of Laurinburg Institute in North Carolina, Scott made a major impact when he was recruited by Larry Brown of the University of North Carolina (UNC), who, along with head coach Dean Smith (who had replaced McGuire in 1961), was committed to integration. Due to Smith's vigilance, Scott became integrated into a resistant Chapel Hill community. Smith accompanied Scott to church and to restaurants, and together, they stared down discrimination. Their courage paid off. Scott grew, as a person and a player, and he was brilliant, leading the team to two Final Four appearances, including a difficult defeat in the 1968 championship to Alcindor's UCLA.

The University of Kentucky was a different story. The Wildcats were led by the legendary Rupp, who had been head coach of the team since 1930 and had led Kentucky to multiple conference championships and four national championships. But Rupp resisted having an African American player on his team until 1969. There is some disagreement over whether Rupp should be called a racist, but the facts speak for themselves: 1969 was twenty-two *years* after Jackie Robinson broke the baseball color line.

By the end of the sixties, the exclusion of black players from a college basketball team should have looked like utter folly. The game had been transformed by African American talent and African American style of play. And it wasn't just UCLA, with Alcindor, Lucius Allen, Mike Warren, and other black stars, that dominated. In 1966, Texas Western College (now known as the University of Texas at El Paso) became the first team with an all-black starting lineup to win a national championship in NCAA basketball. And fittingly, historically, the team they beat in the championship game was the all-white Kentucky Wildcats.

Only one of the Texas Western starters, David Lattin, played professional basketball after college, and his career was modest by any standard. But the collective achievement of these men is out of all proportion to what appeared to be a low-key game that March in 1966. The game was not broadcast live. Texas Western was given no chance by the media. Kentucky was led by future Hall-of-Famers Pat Riley and Louis Dampier. The stands were filled with an all-white audience, some of whom waved Confederate flags.

In his autobiography, *Glory Road*, the Texas Western Miners coach Don Haskins, who had led his squad to a 27-1 record that year, said that he had heard that Rupp had told some people privately that there was no way a black team could beat him. Haskins told his players of this remark in his pregame speech, and his team went out and beat the Kentucky giants 72–65. As Riley recalled, "They were committed and they were more motivated than we were."

This game graphically announced to the world that racism on the court was not just immoral—it was impractical. Black athletes and their innovative style of play were here to stay. It was also a moment of activism. As President Obama put it in 2016, "By becoming the first team to win an NCAA title with five black starters, the Miners weren't just champs on the court: they helped change the rules of the game. They didn't know it at the time, but their contribution to civil rights was as important as any other." In 2006, a movie celebrating the achievement of this game was released, also called *Glory Road*, and the following year, the team was inducted into the Naismith Memorial Basketball Hall of Fame.

Yet to repeat Bill Russell's dictum, we measure progress not by how far we've come, but by how far we have to go. The great college stars and teams of the sixties changed the face of college basketball. For fifty years, we have been thrilled by the brilliance of successive generations of African American athletes on the basketball courts and the football fields of America's colleges. And our thrill and appreciation has created a massive industry—an entertainment machine yielding billions of dollars in revenue and reaching every part of America. Yet the young men and women who generate that wealth, who put their bodies and futures on the line, do so for nothing. In most cases, they do not even emerge from college with a degree. And most of these athletes are African American.

The questions that we must ask about college athletics have changed. It is no longer a matter of African Americans being kept off the court or field, but the conditions by which they are kept *on*. Talking about racism in college sports requires broad thinking. Because it has many layers. Moving past the evolutionary history of exclusion and segregation, we arrive at the hypocrisy of the concept of the "student-athlete," the long and continuing history of corruption, and the matter of exploitation. And there is the money—a lot of money. None of which is going to the athletes who generate it, except in the form of nonmonetary scholarships (where tuition, food, and board are covered, but nothing more).

In 2017, the NCAA, the organization that regulates athletics in many sports for over 1,200 colleges in North America, earned revenues of $1.1 billion. Nearly 80 percent of that figure came from a television rights deal with CBS/Turner Sports for "March Madness"—the annual NCAA college basketball tournament. That deal is worth $8.8 billion and lasts until 2032. But an even larger pile of money is generated by football, the nation's most popular college sport. Because the college playoff championship is owned by the top 125 college teams, those revenues are shared by the colleges themselves rather than the NCAA. And that amount is routinely four times the size of college basketball revenues.

So, the revenues are somewhere between $4 and $5 billion. *Annually*. The predominantly African American athletes who make these billions possible are typically on scholarship. They get their meals and their housing, their tuition, and perhaps a small stipend. Certainly they earn some prestige. But the fleeting glory of a few years of their youth is earned at the expense of their education, which is routinely ignored, as they are exploited for the massive economic value that they bring as athletes. The disparity between their worth and their compensation is so great that several harsh but fair metaphors are often used to describe their situation. Dr. Harry Edwards has called them "gladiators." Professor Billy Hawkins of the University of Houston, a former college athlete himself, has coined the phrase "the new plantation" to describe the system of using talented African American college players to earn huge sums for major universities, while ignoring their low graduation rates when those universities fail to do their primary job: to educate these young men and women.

Hawkins notes that the way in which black athletes are recruited and used at the major colleges in the United States "sustains ideals of scientific racism and reproduces the notion of the physically superior black body similar to how it was represented in the internal colonial system of slavery in North America." The economic and political systems of the NCAA hinder the merging of student and athlete identities. The vast majority of these athletes do not go on to play in the pros, and that fact, combined with low graduation rates, means that the student-athlete ideal is a "dream deferred," which "has cost many black athletes their chances of getting an education, obtaining a college degree, and increasing their chances of social mobility."

Hawkins's language is scientific, but his point is blunt: exploitation. A long, sordid history of black bodies being used for white enrichment. Notably, Abdul-Jabbar has weighed in recently with a similar judgment, calling for fair compensation for college athletes and arguing that "in the name of fairness, we must bring an end to the indentured servitude of college athletes and start paying them what they are worth." He has also argued for the unionization of college athletes and drawn a comparison of the multimillion-dollar salaries of the top coaches and the president of the NCAA with the chief executive officers (CEOs) of powerful corporations, who make even more lucrative salaries while paying foreign workers a few cents an hour to make shoes or shirts.

As magnificent as Abdul-Jabbar's college career was, his twenty-year career in the NBA—six with the Milwaukee Bucks and fourteen with the Los Angeles Lakers—established him as a player who could be better than anyone else, for longer than anyone else. He won six NBA championships, was an All-Star nineteen out of the twenty seasons he played, and retired as the leading scorer in history, with 38,387 points. His consistency was outstanding, as evidenced by the fact that he won championship rings as young as twenty-four and as old as forty. He was without peer.

Time has been good to Abdul-Jabbar, granting him not just the health and talent to compete for as long as he did, but the scope to grow intellectually and spiritually as well. And America has benefited from this growth. His evolution from angry young man to wise elder has seen him turn from a philosophy of separatism to one of inclusion. In his book *Black Profiles in Courage*, he wrote, "We have to empower our young people— especially African Americans who are largely unaware that other African Americans played key roles in *creating* this nation. We need to help them feel they are part of this country and will always *want* to be part of it. It's our common heritage as Americans."

Yet Abdul-Jabbar also teaches us that understanding our own history of unfairness and discrimination can give us the empathy to see injustice elsewhere. Mindful that his mother, Cora, was part Cherokee, Abdul-Jabbar was driven to investigate the long and tragic history of the treatment of Native Americans. Typically, he followed up this study with action, taking a coaching position for a year at a high school on White Mountain Apache Reservation and then writing a book about it afterward. He has also made the effort necessary to grasp the experience of Japanese Americans who were placed in prison camps during World War II in his adopted home of California. "This was something I understand," he has said. "But I believe white Americans struggle to understand things like this. We all, blacks and whites, need to go the extra mile. Or ten to get that point across. It isn't about being stupid or being evil. But some things are hard to understand."

Abdul-Jabbar has extended and refined the tradition of African American athletic leadership in two crucial ways: first, by longevity (fifty years of activism and counting); and second, by adapting his message as he has gone along, becoming more inclusive and more vocal in addressing all Americans about the need for racial justice. Just as he refined his playing style many times over his career, so has he adapted his leadership style. And he has not forgotten history: Who came before; who taught him the lessons of leadership that he has built on. His father. John Wooden. His teammates. And Bill Russell, who occupies a special place in that personal history. "I'm indebted to Bill in so many ways," he has said. "He taught me how to play the game. How to conduct yourself off of the court, and taught me how to communicate understanding between the races. That it isn't done through force, nor by attacking. Bill is calm and civilized."

Abdul-Jabbar likes to retell Russell's own story of growing up poor in Louisiana and then moving to Oakland. When they arrived in their new home, Russell's mother took him around the new city, until they got to the library. She pointed the building out to him and told him that this was where he would be spending a lot of his time. "It was the first time he had seen one," Abdul-Jabbar commented. "He hadn't known what it was. In the segregated South, he never had a library." As a published author with a broad range of interests, Abdul-Jabbar knows the value of a library. Of education. For him, they are keys to liberation.

When Abdul-Jabbar arrived at UCLA from New York City, at nineteen years old, his reputation preceding him, he sat down for a long meeting with Coach Wooden. Wooden was already a legend. He had been head

coach of the Bruins for eighteen years and had won two national championships. He was a recognized basketball genius. So the young Lew Alcindor was surprised when basketball wasn't even mentioned during that meeting. Instead, Wooden talked only about academics. What the young man didn't know was that his new coach was as intimidated as he was. Wooden knew what a prodigy Alcindor was, and was uncertain of how to best use his skills on the basketball court. Of course, Wooden was a man of fierce integrity who truly cared about making sure that his charges were prepared not just for basketball, but for life. So the discussion about education was natural and meaningful.

Time and study and the wisdom they confer have given Abdul-Jabbar the confidence to confront the establishment and to lead by word and

Post-basketball, Kareem Abdul-Jabbar has become one of the nation's most passionate and vocal advocates for social justice and racial equality—in print and in person.

example. A casual look at the myriad books and articles he has written show how broad his knowledge and passions extend: sports, racial justice, history, black culture, and much more. And this range of curiosity and self-expression has equipped him to give us sound advice about how we can all work together to effect change.

In response to the question of how white people can possibly comprehend the experiences of African Americans, he has said, "You listen. You try to empathize." And like President Obama, he points to the strength and timelessness of American institutions as a way of seeking inclusiveness, fairness, and cooperation. "This is the beauty of the Constitution," he has said. "It's made it possible to have a morality we can all agree with. The Constitution and the Bill of Rights exist to enable all faiths and colors to agree with what is right and what is wrong, lawful or unlawful, despite differences of religious backgrounds. It's why America gets things done, and why we have to include everybody, and work toward that end."

STANDING ON THE SHOULDERS OF GIANTS
Althea Gibson and Arthur Ashe

7

NELSON MANDELA, when he was released after twenty-seven years in prison, was asked whom he wanted to meet first. Without hesitation, he said, "Arthur Ashe." The fact that one of history's greatest liberators would ask to see an African American tennis player in such circumstances tells you something. One great leader recognizing another, recognizing the common cause of oppression and a commitment to racial justice. Arthur Ashe took the challenge of fighting racism to a global level. He helped create change that fundamentally altered nations.

On the tennis court, Ashe's career was an evolution from caution to resourcefulness. He achieved greatness by adapting his style of play to the demands of the moment: his opponent, the playing surface and conditions, and his own strengths and weaknesses given his age and physical makeup. He brought a similar growth and adaptability to all parts of his life. As Ashe was a fundamentally shy and careful person, the road to activism and leadership was a long one for him. But, as in tennis, he succeeded brilliantly, fulfilling his goal (in spite of dying far too young) of leaving what the historian Raymond Arsenault calls "a legacy of independent vision and moral purpose that transcended the world of sports."

Growing up in segregated Richmond, Virginia, Ashe faced the challenges that all African American athletes of his generation did. But when he chose to pursue excellence in tennis, he added another layer of difficulty. Unlike boxing, track, baseball, football, and basketball, tennis did not have a deep tradition of participation by black people, certainly prior to the fifties. Like golf, tennis was historically a "white" sport, played mostly in private country clubs in prosperous suburbs far from African American neighborhoods. And country clubs were even slower than most American institutions to overcome discriminatory practice. Until the passing of targeted antidiscrimination laws, country clubs, because they were private, could bar anyone they wanted for ethnic, racial, or religious reasons, or because they were women. And these clubs hosted important tournaments on the tennis circuit, so promising African American players who couldn't play there were disadvantaged in many ways, including their inability to earn the circuit points required to play in the US National Championship (now the US Open) at Forest Hills.

This de facto segregation of amateur tennis is a big reason why, until recently, we have seen few African Americans in the history of the sport—and why Ashe's achievement is so noteworthy. But early on, Ashe did have one distinct advantage. Learning his craft when he did, in the late fifties and sixties, he had the immediate example and inspiration of a black woman who had broken through critical barriers thanks to the sheer force of her talent and persistence: Althea Gibson, the "Jackie Robinson of tennis."

Fifteen years older than Ashe, Gibson was the first African American to compete in a Grand Slam tennis tournament, and the first to win one when she took the French Open title in 1956. Gibson would go on to win ten more Grand Slams (in singles, women's doubles, and mixed doubles), including three Wimbledon and two US Open singles titles. The impact of her achievement was far-reaching. Although it would take more than forty years for another African American woman to win a Grand Slam, the history was not forgotten: not long before Serena Williams won her first US Open title in 1999, she faxed a letter and a list of questions to Gibson. It was significant recognition.

Gibson was a force from a young age, but by the late forties, when she was ready to take on the best in the world, the private-club ban had kept her from getting the points she needed to compete at the US Nationals. That she had been able to compete at all was thanks to the American Tennis Association (ATA). The oldest African American sports organization in the

United States, the ATA did for black tennis players what the Negro leagues did for baseball: create structure and support for African American competition in a segregated society. Gibson was so dominant within black tennis that the ATA lobbied intensely for her to be invited to the 1950 US Nationals. Their cause was helped by a former women's champion—Alice Marble—who wrote a supportive editorial in *American Lawn Tennis* magazine (at that time, the US Open was played on grass). At age twenty-three, Gibson got her invitation, and she played in the US Nationals tournament that summer. Two years later, she played in her first Wimbledon, making it to the third round. Working the national and international circuits hard, she continued to improve until her glory years of 1956–1958, when she won all her Grand Slam titles, after which she retired from amateur tennis.

Althea Gibson's success in the white-dominated world of tennis in the 1950s earned her the title of "the Jackie Robinson of tennis."

Althea Gibson returns to the US victorious. Gibson was the first African American athlete to win a Grand Slam tournament when she won the French Open singles title in 1956.

Gibson paved the way for Ashe, but her link with him was more than simply inspirational. An important mentor for her was the Virginia doctor Walter Johnson, known as "the godfather of black tennis." Johnson had solid coaching ability and an eye for talent. Just as important, he had the skills and resources to create, within the ATA, a development program for young black players and to arrange facilities for them for practicing and playing. Johnson gave Gibson her start within the world of black tennis. He also mentored Ashe. From 1953, when Ashe was ten years old, to 1960, Ashe attended a summer tennis camp that Johnson ran in Lynchburg, Virginia. As Gibson was taking the world by storm, Ashe was patiently honing his skills in a state where he was not allowed to play against white competitors.

In the embattled sixties, when young, ambitious African Americans had to choose where on the activism spectrum they wanted to focus, Ashe was distinctly conservative and cautious. From his father and Johnson, both proud and careful men, he learned that etiquette and sportsmanship were the road to dignity. Johnson told the young Arthur to return every ball, even if it was inches long, and never to argue with an umpire's call. He taught him to avoid controversy. He could see that Ashe had the talent to compete at the highest level, as well as the temperament to deal with bigotry and not let it derail his game.

As a high school student, Ashe won the National Junior Indoor Championships and earned a scholarship to UCLA. At college, he stayed within the lines. He joined a fraternity. He was a member of the Reserve Officer

Training Corps (ROTC) at a time when many young people were demonizing the military. He was also a diligent student, who would graduate with a bachelor's degree in business administration. But study and officer training did not affect his commitment to tennis. His path to greatness continued, as he won an NCAA national singles title and, in 1963, became the first African American player selected for the US Davis Cup team. After graduation in 1966, while Muhammad Ali was battling the establishment by refusing to be drafted, Ashe joined the US Army.

Later in life, as he wrote about Nelson Mandela, Ashe would ask these searching questions:

> Can we African Americans emerge from the prison house of our history with true dignity, as he did—that is, with a determination to remain free, but also without bitterness or any other compromise in our moral principles? Can we prevent our outrage at the wrongs we have suffered in America from destroying our spirit, from depriving us from the high moral ground we once held? Can we avoid the temptation to sink utterly into despair, cynicism, and violence, and thus become abject prisoners of our past?

This language is very different from the rhetoric of Ali or Harry Edwards. It is nuanced and evenhanded. It places a high value on personal dignity. It insists on occupying the moral high ground. And it is typical of the thoughtfulness and care that characterized Ashe's temperament throughout his life. His evolution as an activist and leader emerged from his search for answers to these questions.

Another way in which tennis was different from most popular sports was that until 1968 and the beginning of the so-called Open era (i.e., professional players could compete with amateurs), it was a completely amateur pursuit, with no prize money. Like the Olympics and college athletics, tennis had an amateur code that argued that professionalism would somehow sully the purity of the game. This attitude had its roots in tennis's aristocratic beginnings (similar to golf). Of course, this difference made it all the harder for athletes from poor communities to excel: only people with alternative sources of wealth could afford to devote all their time to tennis. Althea Gibson retired in her prime because she had to make a living. And Arthur Ashe saw the army as a way to continue his tennis career while serving his country and drawing a salary.

Because he was in the army, and because he wanted to maintain his Davis Cup eligibility, Ashe did not immediately turn pro when tennis became "open," and he won his first major, the 1968 US Open, as an amateur (Ashe received $280 to cover expenses; the $14,000 in prize money was actually given to the man he had beaten—Tom Okker, who was a pro). This Grand Slam victory, achieved when Ashe was twenty-five, firmly established him as one of the world's best, a level of excellence he was to sustain for the next decade, earning two more Grand Slam titles—the Australian Open in 1970 and his sweetest win of all, his victory in the 1975 Wimbledon final over his polar opposite, the volatile and mercurial Jimmy Connors.

Tennis success brought Ashe international fame and the opportunity and expectation of leadership. His life choices, his focus on patriotism and self-reliance, and his careful nature put him at odds with many activists of the time, who preached about Black Power and confrontational politics. At times, Ashe resented the expectation that he was a spokesman for his race—but his arguments were always carefully reasoned and defensible. It has been suggested that his activism for racial justice abroad—in Haiti and South Africa—was easier for him because it was a less ambiguous commitment than working for civil rights at home, at least in the early years. But what is fascinating about Ashe is how he matured on his political journey, and how his South African activism in particular led him to a firmer understanding of the challenges facing African Americans.

Another vital factor in Ashe's political development—and one that made him an intersectional figure—was his health. In 1979, at the age of thirty-six and in peak athletic shape, Ashe suffered a heart attack. His family had a history of cardiovascular disease, and tests showed that his arteries were in such bad condition that he needed quadruple bypass surgery, which he hoped would allow him to return to professional tennis. But the surgery was not fully successful, and he needed further corrective surgery in 1983. This effort at correction appeared to succeed, but a few years later, he tested positive for the human immunodeficiency virus (HIV). Blood transfusions that he had received during the second surgery had been infected with the virus.

In 1968, a crucial year in the history of American sports, Arthur Ashe made his own history by being the first African American male to win the US Open and the first player to win both the Open and the national amateur championship in the same year.

Although Ashe chose to keep his condition private—until he was forced to disclose the fact against his will, to preempt it being revealed to the public in *USA TODAY* in 1992—having the disease caused him to rethink and broaden his activist agenda, which is best expressed in his autobiography, *Days of Grace*, published just months after he died in 1993, at not yet fifty years of age. As an AIDS sufferer, Ashe saw himself not as a victim, but as a patient. This conservative man developed great empathy for the gay community, which was being ravaged by AIDS, and counseled gay men without judgment. He became a leading spokesman for AIDS education, frequently speaking on college campuses even though he was deathly ill.

So, late in his short life, Ashe's quiet leadership extended well beyond the challenges faced by the African American community—and well beyond the United States. As Nelson Mandela's admiration confirmed, Ashe's commitment to justice in South Africa had an international effect. In the late sixties and early seventies, when Ashe was in his prime, the all-white South African government was trying to maintain its apartheid social system, while at the same time rejoining the so-called family of nations. In particular, it wished to end its Olympic ban, which had begun in 1964. Ashe had visited the country in the early seventies and seen the injustice—as bad as the worst of Jim Crow in the American South—and decided that the best way of fighting the system was from within, rather than via boycotts. In that spirit, he sought and received a visa to play in an integrated South African Open (he had been refused a visa in 1969), and he played in that tournament in 1973 and 1974, believing that his presence would have a positive influence and help extend that integration to all parts of society.

Typical of his openness and his willingness to learn, Ashe soon discovered that his participation was the wrong approach. And his education on the issue was firsthand. At the integrated tournament, he had tried to buy tickets for some young Africans and was told to use an "Africans only" counter. Shocked, he came to recognize that boycotting was actually the best way of putting pressure on the apartheid regime, and he also called for them to be expelled from the professional tennis circuit and Davis Cup competition. He worked with TransAfrica, a think tank set up by the Black Congressional Caucus and headed by his childhood friend Randall Robinson, and in 1985, he was arrested for protesting outside the South African embassy in Washington. He was also arrested for a similar protest, in 1992, against the US deportation of Haitian refugees.

Nelson Mandela would not forget Ashe's commitment. There was the request to meet Ashe after his prison release. Then, when Mandela had begun reinserting himself into mainstream society, he was interviewed by the ABC news commentator Ted Koppel. Ashe was in the audience. When Mandela heard he was there, he walked over to Ashe and hugged him, calling him "my brother."

But what about Ashe's commitment to racial justice at home? No one questioned him more than he did himself. As he asked in his autobiography:

> To what extent was I trying to make up, with my antiapartheid crusade, for my relative inaction a decade or more earlier during the civil rights struggle? Should I have done more? It was hard for me to act when I could see that what some people wanted me to do would have clashed violently with the principles I had evolved for myself over the years, principles having to do with a love of peace, morality, moderation, and religion. My character was set in this way, and I would not change for anybody.

The focus on self-reliance lay at the root of his disagreement in the eighties with Georgetown basketball coach John Thompson, who was steadfast in his belief that college admissions tests were biased against African Americans. Ashe argued that a black athlete must not expect to be entitled to a scholarship without making an effort to earn it in an academic setting—something that he believed deeply was the reason for his rise to success. He had been able to survive the innumerable trials of segregation. He wished for black athletes to draw upon a comparable inner strength, despite imposed barriers. The belief in education was a logical stance resulting from his close involvement with the United Negro College Fund.

But the dissimilar approach did not prevent Ashe from radically making a difference. His self-questioning resulted in an effort to make up for what he later thought was insufficient activism in his early years. Although AIDS caused his premature departure from playing, as it did for Magic Johnson, Ashe used his visibility as an athlete as a platform to support the African American community. In 1966, when he joined the army, he had publicly stated about Vietnam that "he would be proud to serve in the war." By late 1968, he had changed his attitude. Although he remained an advocate for patient change, he argued that the war and the treatment of the black community were no longer acceptable. He argued that black athletes had to make a commitment to their community and attempt to transform it. He cited his boyhood hero, Jackie Robinson, as well as Bill Russell's willingness to march in Selma. And he aligned himself firmly with the nonviolent philosophy of Dr. King.

Yet he remained a patriot, in the best sense of the word. "Segregation and racism made me loathe aspects of the white South," he wrote, "but had left me scarcely less of a patriot. In fact, to me and my family, winning a place on our national team would mark my ultimate triumph over all those people who had opposed my career in the South in the name of segregation." *Our national team.* These are important words, because the Davis Cup meant more to Ashe than to perhaps anyone else in tennis history. And it also helped him better understand the concept of race and how it operated in mainstream American culture.

Like golf's Ryder Cup, the Davis Cup, which has been an annual international event since 1900, takes an individual sport and turns it into a team sport. It also gives players the added incentive of playing for their country. As such, it was the perfect vehicle for Ashe, who over his career played in thirty-two Davis Cup singles matches and won twenty-seven of them. He was chosen for the squad for ten seasons, five of which resulted in an American championship. Furthermore, when his playing days were over, he captained the team for six more years, two of which resulted in championships. It was a notable record of achievement.

As Davis Cup captain from 1981–1986, Ashe had complicated relationships with the two greatest players of the era—Jimmy Connors and John McEnroe—relationships that provided real drama to his life story and, in indirect but important ways, helped him better understand the issue of race.

Like Ashe, McEnroe and Connors were fiercely competitive, but unlike Ashe, they had disdain for self-restraint (to put it mildly). Both

were known for their petulant behavior on court, their aggression toward umpires, their tantrums, and their disrespect for the game's governing bodies and rules, written and unwritten. Connors had rubbed Ashe the wrong way for years. "I swear, every time I passed Jimmy Connors in the locker room," Ashe recalled, "it took all my willpower not to punch him in the mouth." Ashe's irritation at Connors's arrogance and unsportsmanlike conduct was exacerbated by competition. In their six meetings, Ashe won only once. But that one victory was the 1975 Wimbledon final, one of the most famous battles in tennis history.

Part of Connors's scorn for the conventions of tennis included his refusal to play in the Davis Cup. In his twenty-four-year career, Connors played in only three seasons of Davis Cup, and none before 1975. The reason? It was partly economic (Davis Cup did not pay) and partly temperamental (Connors was never much of a team player). Ashe made sure that the world knew how he felt about Connors's attitude by walking onto

Wimbledon's Centre Court for the 1975 final wearing his Davis Cup sweat-shirt—with "USA" emblazoned across the front. So the match definitely had a personal dimension. Connors was considered unbeatable, but Ashe crafted a careful strategy of taking the pace out of his own game, thus frustrating Connors, who was excellent at using an opponent's pace against him via fierce counterpunching. Connors was dismantled by this bravura strategy, and Ashe won in four sets. It was a loss that Connors would never forget.

Ashe would ultimately coach Connors as captain of the 1981 and 1984 Davis Cup teams, but he was never impressed by Connors's general lack of commitment to the national team. The younger McEnroe was a different story. Davis Cup meant everything to Mac, and he would play in sixty-nine singles and doubles matches spread over thirteen Davis Cup years. Although they did face each other as players twice in 1978, in the twilight of Ashe's career, the real relationship between the two men was captain-player, where Ashe assumed the authoritarian role of father and McEnroe was the spoiled child. The two often clashed over McEnroe's fiery temper and on-court antics. George Plimpton famously wrote that McEnroe was "the only player in the history of the game to go berserk and play better tennis." Needless to say, Ashe did not appreciate this lack of self-control. He struggled repeatedly to mentor McEnroe and manage his talented charge's behavior—though he would say, after McEnroe had brilliantly led the United States to its second consecutive Davis Cup victory in 1982, "The guy's the most talented player ever to play the game."

In time, McEnroe would mellow and recognize how much he had learned from Ashe and how difficult he had made Ashe's job. But Ashe would also learn—or realize—something essential from McEnroe's bad-boy demeanor. And it had to do with race. Ashe was seen throughout his career as cool and collected. Unruffled. But he had as much anger in him as McEnroe had—in fact, he had much more to be angry about than McEnroe did, given their contrasting backgrounds. Yet Ashe saw that McEnroe could get away with his antics precisely *because* he was white. If Ashe, or any other African American tennis player, had exhibited anything close to the rage of McEnroe or the arrogance of Connors, they would have been labeled a problem and banned from the game. It was an important lesson for Ashe to learn, and it helped him move to a more radical position on race as he became more politically involved in the eighties.

Few athletes have had such a full and engaged career with their chosen sport as Ashe had with tennis. Yet his health issues tore him away from playing when he had many good years left. And his early death deprived the world of many potential years of his wisdom and activism. But Ashe managed to do more in the decade of life he had left after his infection in 1983 than most people would in a lifetime. In addition to his civil rights and global leadership, he wrote for *Time* magazine and the *Washington Post*, commentated for ABC Sports, and worked with a team of researchers for five years to write his three-volume history of African American athletics, entitled *A Hard Road to Glory*.

Published in 1988, comprising 1,200 pages, this collection presents a comprehensive history of black athletes from slavery to the late twentieth century. Conceived when Ashe was teaching a course at Florida Memorial College, the project was pushed into his consciousness when he was looking for research materials about African American athletes and found that virtually nothing existed. "Discrimination, vilification, incarceration, dissipation, ruination, and ultimate despair have dogged the steps of the mightiest of these heroes," Ashe wrote. "And only a handful in the last 179 years have been able to live out their postathletic lives in peace and prosperity." David Halberstam called the book "monumental." The sportswriter Jim Murray said, "The point Ashe makes is, the black athlete didn't just roll out of bed with his ability. He really came from a long line of champions, people who had really worked to perfect and refine natural skills but were lost to history because they took the slave owner's name."

Not only did Ashe make an impact in the present moment, he also, through his writing and teaching, did as much as anyone to define the tradition and educate the world about how history informs the present. As his biographer Arsenault put it, "He embraced a dizzying array of roles beyond his career as a tennis star. Social justice and civil rights activist, athletic administrator, coach, author, historian, teacher, lecturer, philanthropist, entrepreneur, diplomat, and public intellectual—he was all these things and more." It is tempting to wonder what Ashe might have achieved had he lived a full life. Public service seemed to beckon. In his last book, *Days of Grace*, he wrote that he had wanted to pursue a life in political leadership, to run for Congress to represent New York's Eighteenth District. "But my thoughts of running ended with my heart attack in 1979."

As the tennis great Pam Shriver told the *New York Times* after Ashe died, "He brought a level of conscience to the game, whether he was speaking on South Africa or inner-city minorities or exclusionary policies anyplace. Arthur's influence on tennis didn't fade after he left the sport." Nearly thirty years have passed since his death, and still his influence remains powerful. "I have an opportunity to be here because of him," Serena Williams said recently. "It motivated me, reading stories about how Arthur wasn't allowed to play when he was young. Because of what he went through, I have the opportunity to be the best that I can be. He influenced people way beyond tennis."

When Ashe died in February 1993, the first African American governor of his home state of Virginia, Douglas Wilder, ordered state flags to be flown at half-mast. Five thousand mourners passed his coffin in Richmond, where he lay in state—Richmond, where just thirty-five years earlier, the African American high school student had not been allowed to play on the city's indoor tennis courts. This progress from segregation to honor should be celebrated—and Ashe did much in his life to bring it about—but he would be the first to tell us that there was still a long way to go then, and a long way to go now.

SISTERHOOD

Serena and Venus Williams

8

THE CAREERS OF VENUS AND SERENA WILLIAMS read like a fantasy—an unbelievable journey from the tough streets of Compton, California, to unprecedented tennis dominance, huge wealth, and global influence. As African Americans, as women, and as athletes who embraced their immense talent and fought their way to the peak of their profession against overwhelming odds, the Williams sisters have thrilled and inspired us. But from the beginning, their achievements have been under the microscope of race in a way that has created challenges for them that fame and fortune have not dispelled. And a large part of their legacy will be the courage that they have shown in handling those challenges and in setting an example of leadership and resolve that will encourage and motivate African Americans, women, mothers, and anyone else who faces the challenges of conscious and unconscious bias.

Althea Gibson and Arthur Ashe laid the groundwork for what the Williamses achieved, both before and after the sisters debuted professionally in the mid-nineties. The link is clear, and acknowledged by both

Venus and Serena, who have always been vocal about the sacrifice and accomplishment of the pioneers who came before them. Gibson and Ashe proved that black tennis players could compete at the highest level, overcome prejudice and skepticism, and become positive role models in a sport that historically has failed to support African American participation.

The example was especially important in the sisters' early years, when their father, Richard Williams, would bring them to practice on public courts on Compton Boulevard, which were surrounded by battered cyclone fencing and the grit and poverty of a city known at the time for its crime and gang activity. Richard had a vision for his girls that seemed foolhardy and impossible to everyone but him. In time, their talent would convince even the most skeptical observers, but in those years, they were just a couple of local girls, dressed in jeans rather than tennis whites, accompanied by their driven father, impressing only folks who stopped to have a look, including many gang members who watched over the girls as they practiced and made sure that they were protected from harassment.

The bigger the tennis challenge, the greater the effort these young women exerted. The stats speak for themselves: Venus and Serena won the first of their fourteen doubles Grand Slams at the 1999 French Open. That same year, at the age of seventeen, Serena won the US Open singles title. It was the first Grand Slam final singles appearance by either her or Venus. Over the next twenty years, covering eighty Grand Slam events, there was a Williams sister in the singles final *forty-nine times*. Over half the finals for two decades. And in nine of those finals, much as they disliked doing so, they faced each other.

However you look at it, the Williams sisters changed the paradigm of professional tennis forever. A case—perhaps a definitive case—can be made for Serena being the greatest tennis player of all time, but the fact that her older sister shared her dominance, and that they are best friends who hated facing each other because one of them had to lose—these details give their story a fairytale dimension that resonates across all cultures.

Sisterhood: Serena (left) and Venus Williams have dominated women's tennis for two decades while pushing boundaries on equal pay for women, rights for working mothers, and a range of other social issues.

You would expect that the rise of such ferocious talents from such humble and difficult beginnings would have created a sense of welcome and exhilaration among people who follow big-time tennis in the United States. After all, what better way to spread the word about the inclusiveness and marketability of this sport than to have such a distinctive, talented, and attractive a pair as the Williams sisters as brand ambassadors? Yet just as Tiger Woods encountered envy, resentment, and bigotry when he invaded the white bastion of professional golf with his outrageous talent, so did Venus and Serena meet barriers created by the tennis establishment—as if their rise to the elite ranks of the sport wasn't hard enough.

In 2001, when the sisters had established themselves as powerhouses on the circuit and had won three Grand Slam singles titles between them, they were at the center of an incident at the Indian Wells Masters tournament that caused them to boycott the event for the next fourteen years.

Indian Wells is one of the biggest non–Grand Slam tournaments in the world, part of the Grand Prix Super Series that ranked players are required to participate in. Over 15,000 spectators and the cream of the world tennis crop typically come to this premier event in its exclusive stadium in Southern California.

Venus and Serena were scheduled to face each other in the semifinal when Venus withdrew at the last minute because of tendinitis in her knee. Some opposing players—and many in the capacity crowd—assumed that Richard Williams, who was coaching his daughters at the time, had fixed the withdrawal to increase Serena's chances of winning. The next day, when Serena faced Kim Clijsters in the final, she was savagely and consistently booed. Richard Williams claimed that he was racially insulted as he and Venus took their seats in the stands. It was an ugly incident that humiliated the Williams family and embarrassed match officials.

Serena, only nineteen at the time, won the match, but she spent hours crying in the locker room. Neither she nor Venus would play in this important tournament again until 2015, when Serena played (Venus would return a year later). Serena would later write that "the false allegations—that our matches were fixed—hurt, cut, and ripped into us deeply. The undercurrent of racism was painful, confusing, and unfair."

Much of the resentment was fueled by the way that Richard Williams chose to coach his daughters and deal with the press. He was definitely unconventional, often eccentric, and prone to outbursts of anger or celebration that rubbed traditionalists the wrong way. When Venus beat Lindsay Davenport in the 2000 Wimbledon final, he leaped over the NBC broadcasting booth, shouted "Straight outta Compton!" and danced triumphantly. He could be defensive and abrasive when he thought his daughters were under attack, and he could have an us-against-the-world attitude. Richard, who shared coaching duties with his then-wife and the sisters' mother, Oracene Price, gradually played less of a role in his daughters' careers as they grew into stardom. Yet he and Oracene must be credited with how they envisioned and nurtured the championship potential of Venus and Serena, providing them with not just a career plan (Richard worked that out when each of them was only four years old), but also giving them emotional continuity, helping them to survive a skeptical media, antagonistic crowds, personal tragedy (the murder of their half-sister, Yetunde Price), and the breakup of their marriage.

Venus has spoken of her father's experiences of growing up in the Deep South, when one wrong word could be a matter of life or death. Knowing that history, she appreciates her ability to speak openly. Others have pointed out the hierarchy of values that Richard imparted to his daughters: God, family, education, business, and tennis—in that order. His is a remarkable African American story in its own right.

Racial and gender narratives have always been part of the Williams story. Serena's famous (or infamous) on-court outbursts—the product of her intense competitiveness and the legacy of having to battle in an environment where she has often been judged differently, as a black woman—tend to be assessed differently from the outbursts of white men like John McEnroe. As well as competing on the tennis court, she has also had to fight off-court as well: for gender parity, for equal pay, for the right to be treated by umpires and other tennis officials in the same way as men are treated. As proponents for equal pay for men and women, particularly in the Grand Slams, Venus and Serena have been key figures in turning the tide: since 2001, the French Open, Wimbledon (Venus had the crucial influence here), and the Australian Open have instituted equal prize money for women (the US Open has had equal pay since 1973).

Since becoming a mother in 2017, Serena's focus on her identities' intersectionality and on gender parity have expanded. While pregnant, she wrote an op-ed for *Fortune* magazine, drawing attention to "the long-neglected fact that the gender pay gap hits women of color the hardest." Venus agrees, and has said, "I think there's a lot happening. But there's a lot more that needs to happen around the world with pay discrepancies.

As much as I can be a part of it—I am." Such directness and active participation in core issues are the product of experience. Overcoming challenges leads to activism. "In every stage of my life," Serena wrote, "I've had to learn to stand up for myself and speak out. I have been treated unfairly, I've been disrespected by my male colleagues and—in the most painful times—I've been the subject of racist remarks on and off the tennis court."

The Williams sisters' advocacy for equal employee pay and a fair working environment is part of a tradition of African American athletes who have turned individual grievances into concrete, collective action. Perhaps because the people who run the power structures of professional sports are mostly white, black activists have often been at the forefront of change—they know, more keenly than most, what it is like to be on the outside of a fairness issue. In the early seventies, Curt Flood revolutionized baseball by declining to report to his new team after he was traded, setting into motion a movement that would give players more power in and say over their working lives. Oscar Robertson did something similar for professional basketball players when, as president of the National Basketball Players Association (NBPA), he filed an antitrust suit against the NBA that opened up free agency and led to increased freedom and higher salaries for players.

But the expansion of leadership beyond sports is even more significant. By standing up for black women everywhere—by acknowledging that if it were not for tennis, they would be underpaid and underappreciated themselves—Venus and Serena join the deeper tradition of Muhammad Ali, Kareem Abdul-Jabbar, and others who have used the platform of their sporting notoriety to draw attention to societal issues, and to call out racism where it exists most insidiously—in the institutions and cultural norms of the United States as a whole.

Such leadership requires a certain amount of fierceness, not to mention a willingness not to worry about what people think. Serena in particular has a ferocity on the court that can be very intimidating to opponents.

Her rivalry with Maria Sharapova is legendary. Sharapova emerged as a major player in tennis when, at age seventeen, she upset Serena in the 2004 Wimbledon final. It was only the second time they had played, and from then on, the competition between the two to be the best in women's tennis escalated to their legions of followers, on and off the court, through the media and through lucrative sponsorships.

But in tennis terms, it was no contest. Although Sharapova beat Serena once more later in 2004, at the year-ending WTA Tour Championships, the next eighteen matches over fourteen years belonged to Serena—including victories in three further Grand Slam finals and the gold-medal match in the 2012 London Olympics—before Sharapova broke the streak with a win over Serena at the 2018 French Open. "Serena behaves as if she's the only player out there," Sharapova has said, "the only person who counts. And you? You are a speed bump. You are a zero. Many great players have that mentality. Serena has it more."

Serena has what basketball great K. C. Jones called "total confidence," or what Stanford University psychologist Carol Dweck labels "the growth mindset." She is a woman "who worked hard, who learned how to keep her focus under pressure, and who stretched her abilities beyond her limit when she had to." The 2003 Australian Open semifinal showed her competitive spirit at its most intense. Down 1–5 and two break points to Kim Clijsters in the final set, she rallied to win. Serena does not believe she can lose a match. Ever. "I hate losing more than I love winning," she has said. This is the woman who, when asked at eleven years of age what player she most admired, said, "John McEnroe."

A year and a half older and equally talented, Venus did not have the same fire as her sister. In their early meetings, Venus controlled the action, winning seven of the first ten matches. But Serena soon turned the corner, permanently changing the dynamic when she captured five consecutive majors from 2002 through 2003. When repeated injuries and age seemed to halt Venus's victories in singles in the majors at seven, she became more of a guiding force for her younger sister. Similarly, Venus did not have the on-court meltdowns that have marked Serena's career. In the 2009 US Open semifinal, Serena lost her temper several times in an intense match, verbally attacked the line judge, and was penalized enough points to lose the match. Nine years later, she had a comparable loss of composure at the 2018 US Open, this time in the final against a young finals first-timer, Naomi Osaka.

Of course, passion is a two-edged sword, especially when you have lived with fishbowl scrutiny throughout your professional life. Serena's passion was encouraged by her mother, who taught her daughters to be strong women, as well as her father. Emotions so intense are bound to fizz over now and again, but those incidents must be set against Serena's remarkable record of twenty-three Grand Slams (and counting). And no less a luminary than Billie Jean King has said about Serena's incidents that "screaming and showmanship are part of this game," and while officials are ready to move on after the outbursts of others, "they don't seem to be as willing when it came to Serena."

Billie Jean King's opinion is important here. She has been an outspoken advocate for gender equality and social justice, and as one of the greatest tennis players ever, the winner of twelve Grand Slam titles in singles (and twenty-seven more in doubles and mixed doubles), her viewpoint has tremendous credibility and weight. As a gay woman who lost millions of dollars in endorsements when she was outed in 1981, as a fighter for gender equity in a very different time, and as the woman who beat the proud chauvinist Bobby Riggs in the famous "Battle of the Sexes" tennis match in 1973, watched by 90 million viewers, she understands better than anyone the intersectional pressures faced by a player like Serena. Her Billie Jean King Leadership Initiative works to create inclusive workplaces with equal pay and to encourage self-expression. Long an inspiration to LGBTQ individuals and athletes, she challenges everyone to work toward a more inclusive world.

STYLE AND POLITICS

THE UNIQUE POWER and passion that fueled the Williams sisters' tennis game also informed their choice of clothing. From the early days of their careers, Venus and Serena wore outfits and accessories that showed their pride in their Compton roots: beaded braids, denim, bright colors, and tutu-style tennis skirts. Inevitably, their choices were politicized, attracting nasty comments and even on-court penalties. This opposition was a modern example of what *Elle* magazine has called "skirt theory": historically, the only sports acceptable for women were "ones they could play without wearing pants."

Yet in spite of frequent criticism, the Williams sisters have used fashion as a tool of empowerment. At the 2018 French Open, for example, Serena wore a full-length black catsuit that was not just fashionable, but custom-designed to prevent blood clots—a requirement for Serena after she had clotted dangerously following the birth of her daughter. Tournament officials banned the outfit, calling it "disrespectful," but later, the WTA would change its rules to allow full-body suits. As Billie Jean King put it in a tweet, "The policing of women's bodies must end. The 'respect' that's needed is for the exceptional talent @serenawilliams brings to the game. Criticizing what she wears to work is where the true disrespect lies."

By means of example, as well as in their off-court actions and words, the Williams sisters continue to promote a similar message of inclusivity. Celebrating their identity as black women, without reservation, is part of that message. Oracene Price was always careful never to allow her daughters' identities to be usurped by marketing demands or aggressive agents. She taught them to be proud of being African American and to appear the way they wanted to appear, even if it alienated traditionalists in this conservative sport. Their decorative selections included colorful beads in their hair. "I wanted them to be women of color and be proud of who they are," Oracene said, "and not let anyone make them be ashamed of it. And that was the purpose of the beads: this showed their heritage and where they came from."

These women continue to push the boundaries of inclusivity and fight for justice. After Serena took a fourteen-month maternity leave to have her daughter, Alexis, in 2017 and returned to the tour to resume her career, she had to face the disadvantage of a dramatic drop in the world rankings—from number 1 to number 453. Serena's example inspired the WTA, the ruling body of professional women's tennis, to create a special ranking for mothers, up to three years after the birth of their child. Furthermore, women at WTA tournaments will no longer be penalized "or prohibited from wearing leggings or compression shorts without a skirt, dress, or shorts over them." This is the kind of influence that Serena can bring to bear on policy, and she is not afraid to exercise it.

These changes are accomplishing more than just moving tennis beyond its traditional, hidebound country-club rules; they are real measures of progress, enabled by women who have been disadvantaged because of their gender, race, and (in Serena's case) role as a mother. The tennis achievements of these two women are too numerous to list. But their leadership and outspokenness are equally significant, now and in the future. As Venus said in *The Times* of London back in 2006, as she fought to end the disparity in pay between men and women at Wimbledon, "I believe that athletes—especially female athletes in the world's leading sport for women—should serve as role models. The message I like to convey to women and girls across the globe is that there is no glass ceiling."

INTERSECTIONALITY
Sheryl Swoopes and
Jackie Joyner-Kersee

9

WILMA RUDOLPH AND ALTHEA GIBSON were international figures. They emerged to global stardom during a time when the odds were overwhelmingly against them: as women, as athletes, as African Americans. They helped women everywhere believe that it was possible to achieve at the highest level, in spite of the deck being so heavily stacked against them, and they helped create an environment where women of color have felt empowered to pursue athletic excellence without reservation—whether in the Olympic Games, the WNBA, or on the fields and courts of schools and colleges throughout the country.

What's more, Rudolph and Gibson—as well as countless other pioneering women who braved discrimination to embrace their passion for sports—pushed the process of educating the public about intersectionality, the unique challenges facing black women around the issues of gender, sexuality, motherhood, and physical ability. As the Williams sisters and Billie Jean King would do after them, they made personal sacrifices to create awareness around very personal circumstances that society has been slow to accept—and acceptance continues to be slow.

There is a long list of black female athletes who have continued the battle for equal treatment and have fought perception as they proudly declared their identity. But two women whose athletic careers extended from the eighties into the new millennium are outstanding examples of how African American women continue to push the boundaries of identity and progress: track-and-field star Jackie Joyner-Kersee, named by *Sports Illustrated for Women* as the greatest female athlete of the twentieth century; and college and WNBA standout Sheryl Swoopes, whose bravery on the basketball court and off was best exemplified by her 2005 decision to come out as gay.

Joyner-Kersee's story is like an update of Rudolph's. She too came from a tough southern background. The child of teenage parents, she grew up in East St. Louis, an embattled river and railroad city that had collapsed in the seventies into one of the country's most troubled areas. Violence was never far from Joyner-Kersee's family: her grandmother was murdered, as was her dance teacher. Also like Rudolph, Joyner-Kersee battled physical affliction. As a student-athlete at UCLA in the early eighties, just as she was beginning to reach her world-class potential, she was diagnosed with asthma.

At first, she felt denial about this physical disability: "I was always told as a young girl," Joyner-Kersee has said, "that if you had asthma, there was no way you could run, jump, or do the things I was doing athletically. So, I just knew it was impossible for me to have it. It took me a while to accept that I was asthmatic. It took me a while to even start taking my medication properly, to do the things that the doctor was asking me to do. I just didn't want to believe that I was an asthmatic." But once she understood that the condition was getting in the way of her outstanding athletic gifts, she learned that asthma is a disease that can be managed. And she learned what to do to get it under control.

Yet the disease was always there, which makes the scale of Joyner-Kersee's accomplishments all the more remarkable. Before leaving high school, she participated in the 1980 Olympic trials, where she finished eighth in the long jump. At UCLA, she was a four-year standout on the basketball court. On the track, she continued to develop as a long jumper, but she was inspired to compete in the multidisciplinary heptathlon after watching a movie about the great all-around athlete Babe Didrikson Zaharias, who competed successfully in golf, basketball, baseball, and track and field. Over four Olympiads, from Seoul in 1984 to Atlanta in 1996, Joyner-Kersee won six medals in the long jump and heptathlon, including three golds. She would also take four world-championship golds during that span, as well as four golds at the Goodwill Games. Let's

"The greatest female athlete of the twentieth century": Jackie Joyner-Kersee overcame asthma to become a six-time Olympic medalist, and she remains the world-record holder in the heptathlon.

remember: the heptathlon comprises seven events: the 100-meter hurdles, long jump, high jump, 200-meter run, shot put, javelin, and 800-meter run. It is demanding and grueling, and Joyner-Kersee holds the top six all-time best results in a competitive career that stretched over twenty years. (And she still holds the Olympic record for the long jump.)

And yet always, the asthma was close by. Being an elite athlete made having the disease even more complicated. Many of the best asthma drugs available at the time were banned by the IOC because they were stimulants. Meanwhile, the drugs that she was allowed to take tended to make her sleepy and uncoordinated. She also had to do a lot of international travel, competing in physical environments that could easily bring on an attack. And yet she persisted, and her record of world-class performances speaks for itself.

Like Joyner-Kersee, Sheryl Swoopes was a dominant force in her sport for nearly twenty years. As an unstoppable forward for Texas Tech, she led her college team to the NCAA championship in 1993 and was named Naismith College Player of the Year. A player with great speed and an ability to make quick moves without losing velocity, she set a slew of college records, including the single-game NCAA women's tournament scoring record, with forty-seven points against Ohio State. Not only was she an offensive dynamo, her defense was impeccable. The greatest collegiate player of her era, she went on to become an indispensable part of the Houston Comets WNBA dynasty in the late nineties, winning the league's MVP award three times and being named to the WNBA All-Star team six times. Finally, she was a member of three gold-medal-winning USA basketball teams, at the 1996, 2000, and 2004 Olympics.

These records and achievements would be more than enough to preserve Swoopes's name in the history of American basketball (men's or women's). But mixed into her accomplishments were the realities of a woman's life, including motherhood (she had a child in 1997, near the beginning of her professional career) and her sexuality. Swoopes did not shirk from the challenges these life realities posed for her. And she had a lot to lose. She was the first female basketball player to have a sneaker named after her, through a lucrative contract with Nike. Nike continued the line of "Air Swoopes" after she came out in 2005, and the line is still marketed today.

Indeed, Nike has a progressive record of support for gay athletes; in 2016, for example, when boxer Manny Pacquiao made disparaging comments about gays and lesbians, Nike terminated his endorsement contract. However, gay athletes like Billie Jean King have always been conscious of the impact that coming out may have on their ability to make a living. "Some athletes have this image to uphold and may feel like sponsors won't want them if they're gay," soccer Olympian Megan Rapinoe, who came out in 2012, has said. "I hope that would never go through [sponsors'] minds, but I think it does."

But it's not just about endorsements; it's about professional success in general. It is no coincidence that there are currently no openly gay male athletes in the big four of professional North American sports: MLB, NBA, NFL, and NHL. Those players, now retired, who have come out while active in those leagues, such as NBA player Jason Collins and NFL lineman Ryan O'Callaghan, are on record as struggling with the decision and suffering the hostility that can come from the hypermasculine attitudes prevalent in American sports.

The WNBA seems to offer a more welcoming environment for lesbian and bisexual players, and that is at least partly because of Swoopes's bravery in coming out in 2005. Her declaration may not have created the shock that accompanied Billie Jean King's outing in 1981, but it was courageous and risky nevertheless. The fact that Swoopes had taken maternity leave from the Comets eight years earlier, returning to action only six months after the birth of her son, Jordan, in 1997, and leading them to the WNBA championship that year, also meant that she was used to shattering barriers and balancing her personal identity with her professional life.

THE CHALLENGES OF COMING OUT

JASON COLLINS PLAYED thirteen seasons in the NBA. For twelve of those, he hid a fundamental truth about himself. But then the 2011–2012 season was postponed by a lockout, and he discovered something: basketball, for all those years, had been an outlet that enabled him to ignore the crucial issue of his sexual orientation. With the season suspended, with no basketball, Collins said that his "rhythm was thrown off," and he was forced to confront the fact that being in the closet did not allow him to express his authentic self as a gay man. So, in the spring of 2013, he took a bold step and became the first player in major-league American sports to come out while still an active player. At the time, he was wearing jersey number 98 in honor of Matthew Shepard, the gay teen from Wyoming who had been murdered in a hate crime in 1998. That combination of personal bravery and activist sentiment clarified Collins's sense of purpose, and since retiring after the 2014 season, Collins has worked with the NBA to educate younger players about LGBTQ issues and to make the league more inclusive.

Yet Swoopes's decision was critically different from King's, and from the public announcements by Arthur Ashe (in 1992) and Magic Johnson (in 1991) that they were HIV positive. King, Ashe, and Johnson were prominent figures, with financially secure futures and considerable public cachet. King was arguably the most powerful woman athlete ever, with a gentle personal demeanor that belied her willingness to take on the predominantly male hierarchy in her sport. Also, she is white. Ashe and Johnson, both black, were international superstars—furthermore, their contraction of the AIDS virus occurred via blood transfusion and hetero-

Jason Collins was the first player in major-league American sports to come out while still an active player, and tennis champion Martina Navratilova, who came out as a lesbian in 1981, has called Collins a "game-changer" for team sports.

sexual contact, respectively, as opposed to via gay sex. Their battles were significant and challenging, no question, but their sexual identity has been only an indirect part of their story.

Sheryl Swoopes was in a far less protected position. Because of the secondary status conferred upon women basketball players in the United States, she didn't have the same armor of status—and she didn't have the financial resources either. By 2005, she was divorced, in a relationship with former Comets player and assistant coach Alisa Scott, and broke. But the time was right for her. And she was totally honest about her sexuality. "It doesn't change who I am," Swoopes said. "Discovering I'm gay just happened much later in life. Being intimate with a woman . . . never had entered my mind up until then."

Her decision had a very real effect on the WNBA and how it is marketed. Before Swoopes's coming out, the league had chosen to counter an erroneous, wink-and-nod assumption that women athletes were more likely to be gay than their male counterparts with the promotion of the league as a "straight environment." Because Swoopes had become such an icon of the WNBA, her choice to discuss her sexuality openly and honestly forced the league to become more honest itself. The WNBA stopped being in denial and embraced a more inclusive philosophy, as well as an acceptance—and celebration—that an important portion of its player and fan base is gay. This new approach has been evident in the league's celebration of Pride Month and its support of gay and lesbian issues. It has acknowledged diversity as a strength of the league, understanding that its players are not only athletes and performers, but women with varied and complex personal lives. And Swoopes was key to that transformation. As the writer Summer McDonald has put it, "She was electric. No matter the motive or Swoopes's personal life thereafter, her decision to come out created a less arduous environment for those who came after her."

The WNBA's revised profile certainly has a political dimension. After the Minnesota Lynx beat the rival Los Angeles Sparks in a hard-fought, competitive championship series in 2017, they were not invited to the White House, a traditional courtesy extended to professional championship teams. Lynx coach and general manager Cheryl Reeve told the *Washington Post*, "It's hard not to think that gender is playing a role here because of the consistency with which men's teams are being invited and celebrated. I think it reflects the priorities of this particular administration." On their first team visit to Washington the following season, Lynx players made a point of visiting a local DC school and distributing athletic shoes to kids. As it happened, that visit occurred at around the same time that President Donald Trump disinvited the NFL champion Philadelphia Eagles from visiting the White House—another example of the political establishment's huge gap in understanding how African American athletes are choosing to raise awareness, express protest, and combat discrimination.

Joyner-Kersee's personal story also has a larger, political dimension. During and after her athletic career, she has been a strong and compelling voice for awareness and change. And she has never been afraid of the big stage. In 1998, she appeared on a panel at a town hall meeting on race and sports, initiated and overseen by then-president Bill Clinton and broadcast live on ESPN. In the company of the president of the United States, as well as powerful and forthright men like Jim Brown and John Thompson, the thirty-six-year-old Joyner-Kersee more than held her own on the subject of why African Americans are not better represented in positions of management and ownership. "We can talk and we can talk, but people need to listen, and people need to do something about it," she said, before stating plainly that African Americans are denied senior coaching and management positions because of "subtle racism . . . hidden racism."

More recently, she has become instrumental in changing the conversation around the way that female athletes are perceived by the public. She is conscious of the benefits she received from policy and legislation. Joyner-Kersee had earned a scholarship to UCLA partly because of Title IX of the Education Amendments Act of 1972, a federal law that states, "No person in the United States shall, on the basis of sex, be excluded from participation in, be denied the benefits of, or be subjected to discrimination under any education program or activity receiving federal financial assistance." Today, she speaks out regularly on the need for awareness and legislation as a two-pronged approach to the ongoing battle for women to succeed in athletics and elsewhere.

Yet Joyner-Kersee remains optimistic. "We live in a world where sports have the potential to bridge the gap between racism, sexism, and discrimination," she has said, and after her retirement from track, she established the Jackie Joyner-Kersee Foundation, based in her hometown of East St. Louis, to change the lives of at-risk children throughout the United States through athletic summer camps and other programs. She is also a founding member of Athletes for Hope, which involves athletes in charitable causes and encourages people from all walks of life to volunteer in and support their communities.

Sheryl Swoopes continues to follow her own path. After she and Alisa Scott raised her son together, they separated in 2011, with Swoopes announcing her engagement to longtime male friend Chris Unclesho soon after. There was some inevitable negative reaction in the media (one headline announced that Swoopes was "not so gay after all"), which failed to understand the complexity of identity. As Maya Rupert of the Center for Reproductive Rights has written, "Not every person who has a significant same-sex relationship and a significant different-sex relationship identifies as bisexual. For example, some people who identify as straight previously had same-sex relationships that simply do not affect the way they identify." When it comes to sexual and gender identity, it's best to be open and respectful of what a person is expressing. "It's a mistake to think that we can take a snapshot of a person's relationship at a given moment," Rupert continued, "and assume we can tell their identity."

In this respect, we can continue to learn from Swoopes—and other men and women who have the courage to understand and pursue the often-complicated challenge of identity—about the importance of tolerance and inclusivity, in sports and in society at large.

TAKING CARE OF BUSINESS
Magic Johnson, Michael Jordan, Tiger Woods

10

PROFESSIONAL SPORTS IN AMERICA changed profoundly in the eighties. At the center of the change was money. In 1980, pitcher Nolan Ryan signed a four-year free agent contract with the Houston Astros for $1 million a year. A year later, Magic Johnson signed a twenty-five-year deal with the Los Angeles Lakers, also worth $1 million a year. Other players and other sports followed suit. These numbers may seem small compared to today's massive contracts, but those first million-dollar deals were a sign of a new order. A measure of power had shifted from owners to athletes. Free agency, the brand potential of individual stars, and the reach of television and other media gave professional athletes unprecedented bargaining power.

This change has had a dramatic impact on the national conversation about race. The top stars of the major sports were now extremely wealthy men and women. Added to their celebrity status was massive market influence. The best of them made even more from endorsements than from their huge team contracts. And those endorsements depended on image, shaped by a consumer culture that was mainstream and white. This reality created a quandary for many African American athletes. The highest paid ones tended to have the most potential for leadership and influence. Yet they also had the most to lose, at least financially. Expressing anything but bland opinions could endanger their riches. The United States had evolved to the point where it accepted black people's achievement, especially in the worlds of sports and entertainment (which sometimes meshed together). But most people had yet to accept that institutional racism continued to exist and that prominent black athletes had every right to use their platform to protest that fact.

As a result, African American athletes faced a newer, subtler barrier. On the playing field, they had achieved a hard-earned equality. In the wider world, however, from the front offices of the teams that employed them to the street of the cities and towns where they were born and raised, lack of opportunity, harassment, and double standards continued to be the norm. When these newly minted multimillionaires and household names learned about discrimination, did they call it out and risk appearing "political," or did they stay quiet? Did they make plain their unhappiness with institutional racism, silently work for change behind the scenes, or do nothing at all? Meanwhile, African Americans' resentment at their ongoing second-class citizenship continued to build, breaking out violently decade after decade, ranging from the Miami riots of 1980, to the LA riots that followed the acquittal of the police officers who beat Rodney King, to the postmillennial explosion of anger and civil action in response to police killings of still more black men from Cincinnati to Milwaukee to Ferguson, and beyond.

Three African American athletes who dominated American sports during this period—and have continued to exert tremendous cultural and economic power via their second careers as businessmen—have handled this leadership challenge in different ways. There is no doubting their commercial acumen; today, Earvin "Magic" Johnson, Tiger Woods, and Michael Jordan are among the half-dozen richest athletes of all time, each with an estimated net worth, individually, ranging from $600 million to well over $1 billion. Their talent, influence, and global recognition have led us to expect a great deal of them, in every sphere of life. So it is natural for people concerned about discrimination to ask: What is their record on leadership, activism, and support for the cause of equality? Where do they stand on police brutality and mass incarceration? What are they doing to help?

It's fair to note that leadership can take many forms. A global star like Michael Jordan, by virtue of his athletic accomplishments alone, can be a positive force for African Americans and others, not only because of the grit and discipline and focus that he displayed as he became the greatest basketball player ever, but also because he played in a style that felt, in itself, like a core statement of black culture. MJ taking the ball to the hoop was like a saxophone solo by John Coltrane or a comic riff by Bernie Mac. It didn't just get the job done—it did it in a style that had the swagger and swing and attitude of certain kinds of African American culture. Think Otis Redding or Sam Cooke. Tupac or Kendrick Lamar. Think of the great black preachers.

"There's a reason you call somebody the 'Michael Jordan of...'" President Barack Obama has said. "Because Michael Jordan is the Michael Jordan of greatness."

The same can be said of Magic Johnson, who reinvented the position of point guard and whose joy at playing was as evident as his talent. Both men combined their overwhelming ability and ferocious competitiveness with their unique expression of African American style. It is the style that completely dominates basketball to this day. In spite of the sport's global popularity and the recent influx of international players into the NBA, the world's greatest basketball league is, like jazz, a fundamentally African American institution.

Tiger Woods had a comparable (though more limited) effect in golf. When he exploded onto the professional tour, he brought a level of power, athleticism, and mental focus unseen since the retirement of Jack Nicklaus. Like tennis, golf is historically a white sport with country-club roots, the domain of wealthy suburbanites. In this elite world, opposite in tone and setting to the basketball courts of the inner city, Woods's massive impact was all the more revolutionary. Within a year of turning pro, he had won three PGA Tour events, was ranked number one in the world, and won the Masters, golf's most prestigious tournament, by an amazing twelve strokes (setting a record that still has not fallen). He was twenty years old. And the promise of this magnificent start did not wane. He would go on to win fifteen majors (and counting), second only to Nicklaus, and eighty PGA Tour events, second only to Sam Snead. Also, he was the youngest player (at age twenty-four) to achieve the career Grand Slam and the fastest to win fifty PGA tournaments. In 2019, Woods underlined his talent and competitiveness by winning the Masters for the fifth time—his first major victory in eleven years.

Yet leadership off the basketball court or golf course is a different matter, and in this respect, these three great athletes offer varying legacies. To some extent, their choices are part of an old story: Social activism, or pull yourself up by the bootstraps? Vocal leadership, or do your job and don't make waves? Like Jim Brown, Jordan has been philosophically inclined to encourage black entrepreneurship over social advocacy (although he has also donated many millions of dollars to charity, philanthropy that he practices consistently and humbly, without drawing attention to it). In 2015, Kareem Abdul-Jabbar accused Jordan of favoring "commerce over conscience." And Jordan has had one of the world's most famous brands to protect (namely, Nike). But when does protecting a brand take precedence over taking a stand? Politics is public, but individual political philosophy is very personal, of course, and every athlete makes his or her own decision on the basis of conscience and temperament.

Michael Jordan's personal politics is his own business, and Abdul-Jabbar and other African American commentators have asserted their right to assess how he has used his power and influence to put pressure on the individuals and institutions that perpetuate inequity. In the nineties, when he was at the peak of his achievement and popularity, many activists claimed that he appeared to be more concerned with protecting his sponsors than speaking out against injustice. When Harvey Gantt, the first African American mayor of Charlotte, North Carolina, twice ran against Jesse Helms (who, among other reactionary stands, opposed the Voting Rights Act) for a seat in the US Senate, Jordan, a North Carolina native, did not accede to a request to endorse him, reputedly saying that "Republicans buy sneakers too." At the 1992 Olympics, after the greatest basketball team ever assembled—the "Dream Team," which included Jordan, Johnson, Larry Bird, and others—won the gold medal, Jordan used the American flag to cover the Reebok logo on his warm-up jacket (Reebok, a competitor of Nike, had secured the branding rights to the US Olympic team's warm-up clothing). "I feel very strongly about loyalty to my own company," Jordan said, prompting many to comment that he appeared to value his brand more than he loved his country. The contrast with the black men who protested at Mexico City was frequently noted.

The same questions have been asked of Woods. Although Tiger's mixed-race background has given rise to speculation about his own sense of identity, his father, Earl, was always clear about the issue. Even though Tiger has Thai and Chinese heritage on his mother's side, and Native American, African American, and white on his father's, he was raised African American. His son may have had a variety of ethnicities in his background, Earl has said, "but like I told him: 'In this country, there are only

Tiger Woods (left) is part of an impressive foursome as he is joined on the links by presidents Bush, Clinton, and Obama.

two colors, white and non-white'. And he ain't white." Yet Woods has often been accused of being close-mouthed about social justice issues, even in the Black Lives Matter era, when black athletes have stepped forward in greater numbers to call out police harassment and extrajudicial killings of young black men and women.

This silence, critics argue, extends to the present day. In recent years, Woods would not criticize Donald Trump, nor did he support LeBron James publicly when Trump insulted James's intelligence in a famous tweet. Woods also once ducked the issue of playing in a PGA event in South Carolina while the Confederate flag was still flying at the Capitol, claiming to be going on vacation. Yet Woods has been the victim of racism. As a young man of color crashing the all-white party of golfing success back in the nineties, he was the target of plenty of nasty, racist talk and innuendo. While he was mopping up the field at the legendary 1997 Masters, the pro golfer Fuzzy Zoeller (who finished thirty-fourth) said of Woods, "He's doing quite well, pretty impressive. That little boy is driving well and putting well. He's doing everything it takes to win. So you know what you guys do when he gets in here? You pat him on the back and say congratulations and enjoy it and tell him not to serve fried chicken next year. . . . Or collard greens or whatever the hell they serve." Such language needs no deconstructing.

Like Jordan, Woods hit the endorsement jackpot early, signing deals worth $60 million with Nike and Titleist less than a year after turning pro. From then on, his annual endorsement income was often more than ten times his winnings on the tour. Jordan was also only twenty-one when he signed his first deal with Nike to create the iconic basketball shoe, Air Jordan, a brand that continues to dominate the athletic shoe market more than thirty-five years later. So both men have been living all their professional lives with the pressure of maintaining a consistently neutral image that will not disrupt their principal sources of income.

Although Woods remains quiet, Jordan did go public on the issue of police killings in a 2016 article entitled "I Can No Longer Be Silent." His stance, however, was carefully worded:

> As a proud American, a father who lost his own dad in a senseless act of violence, and a black man, I have been deeply troubled by the deaths of African Americans at the hands of law enforcement and angered by the cowardly and hateful targeting and killing of police officers.

In the article, Jordan announced that he was donating $1 million to both the International Association of Chiefs of Police's Institute for Community-Police Relations and the NAACP Legal Defense Fund. His position was welcomed by the mainstream but criticized by the left for a lack of understanding of conditions on the ground and for expressing his anger only at such a late date.

As a player, however, it is important to note that Jordan's stance was not unusual. Few NBA players chose to protest publicly in the nineties,

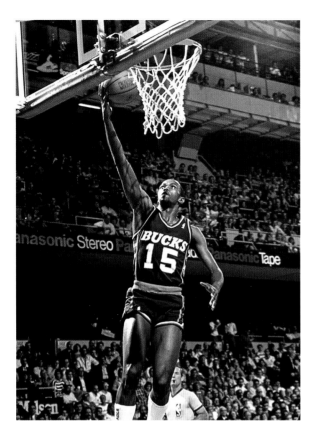

Craig Hodges won the NBA three-point contest three years in a row, but more significantly he was a committed political activist in the mid-1990s, a period when there were few players taking a stand for social justice.

though there were some brave souls who did, when the league and the public had even less appetite for activism than they do today. In 1996, long before Colin Kaepernick took a knee, Denver Nuggets point guard Mahmoud Abdul-Rauf refused to stand for the national anthem before games, declaring that the US flag was a symbol of oppression and the United States had a long history of injustice. (He was suspended by the league without pay.) One of Jordan's teammates, Craig Hodges, was even more pointed in his activism. After the Chicago Bulls won the NBA championship in 1992, Hodges wore a West African dashiki on the team's visit to the White House and delivered a handwritten letter to President George H. W. Bush, complaining of his administration's treatment of people of color. That year, Hodges also called out Jordan for failing to use his fame to draw attention to social and political issues and for "bailing out" when asked for an opinion after the 1992 riots in Los Angeles.

Perhaps Jordan, a billion-dollar businessman and essentially a private person, is uncomfortable with public political confrontation. Perhaps he does not agree that racism is a persistent, deeply ingrained feature of contemporary America. In fairness, that has to be said. In this respect, however, it is interesting to contrast the more inclusive path taken by Magic Johnson—similar in so many ways to Jordan, as a player and as a businessman, and yet with some crucial differences.

CRAIG HODGES WOULD PAY a price for his activism. A two-time NBA champion and winner of the NBA's Three-Point Contest three years in a row, he was a solid journeyman in the league for ten years. However, after delivering a letter to President George H. W. Bush in 1992 protesting the treatment of people of color by his administration, he did not play another minute in the NBA. Soon after that, he was waived by the Bulls and, like Colin Kaepernick twenty-five years later, could find no other NBA team even willing to give him a tryout. He filed a $40 million lawsuit against the league, alleging that the Bulls had released him because of his political outspokenness. But in those less-than-enlightened times, the suit went nowhere. "I never considered I'd be ostracized," Hodges said in 1996. "I was taught during the civil rights era to talk up for what's being right. Stand up, be dignified. That's what I learned from Muhammad Ali and Paul Robeson."

One important difference is personal history. In November 1991, just as AIDS became the leading cause of death in the United States among men aged twenty-five to forty-four, Johnson declared that he was HIV positive and announced his retirement from professional basketball. It was a stunning piece of news. Like Arthur Ashe, Johnson, who picked up the virus via heterosexual contact, had firsthand experience with a disease that was ravaging the gay community. Even though Johnson was not gay, the disease led him to a sympathy for the gay minority that he has maintained ever since. When Johnson's son came out as gay in 2013, Magic was publicly and vocally very supportive. He has also been active in AIDS education, especially in African American communities, which the disease hits disproportionately.

Whether because of this medical condition or for other reasons, Johnson has a record of public leadership and activism that contrasts with the relative silence of Jordan and Woods. He is not just outspoken; his philanthropy and business interests have a multicultural dimension that is more than just rhetoric and inspiration—they also deliver real and practical benefits to the African American community, especially in the Los Angeles area. That vision started early. Fighting off the despair of having his basketball life taken away at age thirty-two, Johnson dedicated his second career to building up his financial interests, incrementally constructing Magic Johnson Enterprises, a collection of businesses that foster community and economic empowerment and promote minority businesses. Using the power of his brand, the company forms partnerships that create job opportunities, reshape corporate understanding of urban areas, and raise awareness.

Johnson's vision is uniquely of the twenty-first century. He has combined Bill Russell's frank challenging of the establishment with Jim Brown's emphasis on helping underprivileged people. It is a vision that is both progressive and practical. Like other NBA stars who have built up business empires after their playing careers were over, such as Junior Bridgeman and Vinnie Johnson, Johnson has been creative in searching for business solutions that grow his empire while simultaneously benefiting the African American community. Allied to that creativity is an awareness of social issues that, as a wealthy man, he has not had to deal with for his adult life. It is easy to forget the past. Johnson has not.

"Equality, diversity, and inclusion" are the watchwords for Johnson. They express the core values of his business and of his life. In 2018, when Donald Trump tweeted an insult about LeBron James—"LeBron James was just interviewed by the dumbest man on television, Don Lemon. He made LeBron look smart, which isn't easy to do"—the same tweet that Michael Jordan refused to weigh in on (at least initially), Johnson responded right away, saying that Trump should focus on his job and

Earvin "Magic" Johnson has made his mark as a player, sports executive, and head of Magic Johnson Enterprises, an investment company focused on supporting urban business and equal opportunity.

learn about the importance of inclusiveness. "Stay focused on North Korea, job creation, what this country needs," Johnson advised. "You can't take away, whether it's a player or an individual, freedom of speech. And you have to be in touch with why everybody is protesting . . . the fact that there are issues in urban America, which I've been dealing with for thirty years."

Johnson thinks globally but is also focused on his adopted home of Los Angeles. Originally from Lansing, Michigan, he grew up in a close family with parents who instilled a deep work ethic in all their children. Magic (his birth name is "Earvin") went to high school during the time when federally mandated busing was seen as part of the solution to de facto segregation. Instead of attending the predominantly black Sexton High School, which was five blocks from his home, he was bused to the predominantly white Everett High School. The change was difficult. There were racist taunts and challenges when he joined the basketball team. At first, Johnson resisted the change, but he learned to persevere; later, he would say that having to attend Everett "got me out of my own little world and taught me how to understand white people, how to communicate and deal with them." Needless to say, he was also great for the high school, leading them to the Michigan state championship in 1977.

But even after his long career with the Lakers, Los Angeles would be his home. He was there during the Rodney King crisis and subsequent riots in 1992. And he was still there twenty-five years later, when someone spray-painted the n-word onto the front gate of LeBron James's LA house. The incident happened just a few months after Johnson had assumed the role of president of basketball operations for the Lakers. "We know there's [still] a racial divide," he said. "If something like this can happen to LeBron James's house, it can happen to everyone. These things need to stop. We need to do something about it." James was even more pointed. "No matter how much money you have, no matter how famous you are, no matter how many people admire you, being black in America is tough," he said. "We have a long way to go for us as a society and for us as African Americans until we feel equal in America."

When we think of Magic Johnson, we see him in a purple-and-gold Lakers jersey. He *is* Los Angeles. In addition to his ownership stake in the Lakers, he owns pieces of the Los Angeles Dodgers, Major League Soccer's Los Angeles FC, and the WNBA's Los Angeles Sparks. And he sees himself as one of the custodians of one of the greatest traditions in professional sports—the Lakers have won sixteen NBA championships and been the home of many of the greatest in the game, including Jerry West, Elgin Baylor, Wilt Chamberlain, Kareem Abdul-Jabbar, Shaquille O'Neal, and Kobe Bryant. So it seemed like a natural move for Johnson to take on the role of president of basketball operations for the Lakers in 2017.

Before assuming that leadership role, Johnson had spent years developing a business plan for the city of Los Angeles. That kind of local loyalty impressed LeBron James, who has invested heavily in his home region of Northeast Ohio. So when LeBron became a free agent in 2018 and every team in the NBA was vying for the services of the best player in the league—at this time, and perhaps ever—Johnson made a typically bold move, signing James to a four-year deal. They were kindred spirits. For business reasons, for the love of the game, and as a student of basketball history, with specific foresight into the opportunities that Los Angeles could bring his growing media career, LeBron saw Johnson's vision for him and left Cleveland, his home, to join the Lakers.

Johnson's tenure as Lakers president, however, was short-lived; in 2019, he resigned, expressing a wish to return to his role as an NBA ambassador. Yet the vision of men like Johnson and James has had an effect on the NBA. The league is a progressive institution, partly because of the vision of its commissioner, Adam Silver, who has been attentive to the leadership of Johnson and others. Under Silver's stewardship, the league has a much improved record on diversity, equality, and inclusiveness. The NBA was the first of the four major professional sports leagues to employ a female assistant coach (San Antonio Spurs assistant Becky Hammon), and it transferred its All-Star Game out of Charlotte in 2017 after North Carolina passed anti-LGBTQ legislation. When Los Angeles Clippers owner Donald Sterling was captured on tape making racist comments, Silver banned him from the NBA for life and fined him $2.5 million.

There is no doubt that, for the NBA if not the NFL, athlete activism is having a positive institutional effect. And that impact shows signs of spreading into the corporate world. Magic Johnson recently lamented refusing an offer of stock in Nike in 1979 (he endorsed Converse instead). Nike has since grown into one of the world's most iconic brands, valued in excess of $29 billion and a powerful influence in shaping the image not just of Jordan, Woods, and James, but of countless other athletes, from Serena Williams to Kyrie Irving. On Labor Day 2018, Nike announced the new face of its brand, tweeting an image of Colin Kaepernick, the African American athlete most associated with the activist campaign to protest police brutality by kneeling or sitting during the national anthem. Nike's tweet featured a photograph of Kaepernick staring directly at the camera.

Overlaid text read: "Believe in something. Even if it means sacrificing everything. Just Do It [Nike's famous slogan]."

The new campaign caused a social media storm, with responses largely following political lines. Some welcomed Nike's embrace of the controversial athlete and his beliefs; others saw it as an endorsement of someone who was disloyal to the American values of patriotism and respect for the flag. But a third stream of opinion argued that Nike had coopted protest and resistance to build a brand—that the company's mission to sell shoes was cynically leveraging Kaepernick's political platform and publicity.

Has activism in this case been commodified? Is there a fundamental contradiction between the goals of business and the goals of politics? Why are so many people comfortable with athletes selling things, but uncomfortable with them making political statements? These are questions that the rise of superwealthy athlete-businessmen like Johnson, Jordan, and Woods has made many ask, especially in the African American community. How those questions are answered will be a big part of how athlete activism will develop in the future.

RIDING WITH THE KING
LeBron James

11

LEADERSHIP STARTS with holding yourself accountable, in *any* area of life. You cannot demand sacrifice and courage of others unless you have displayed those virtues yourself—consistently, wisely, and without ego.

On the court, field, park, or rink, the issues are clear. You are there to win, while respecting your opponent and the rules of the game. The greatest athletic leaders are those who inspire and guide their teammates by word and deed to achieve that goal. However, once you have taken off the uniform, once you are back in the real world with all its nuanced conditions and social complexities and historical realities, your leadership challenge becomes much more difficult. No one is going to tell athletes that they shouldn't try to win. But in the arena of politics, on the streets and in the institutions of power, there will always be those who want to preserve the status quo, no matter how unfair it may be to the minority. There will always be those who want you to stay out of politics and play ball.

Charles Barkley—master of reinvention and former NBA MVP—once predicted that with the exponential rise of salaries in professional sports during the first two decades of the new millennium, black athletes would be in a strong position to rededicate themselves to activism. What was needed was leadership. What was needed was consciousness of the public problems that demanded to be addressed, as well as a cadre of men and women with a platform of influence and the courage and judgment to call out the causes of those problems, knowing that many in society will tell them to "shut up and dribble."

The problems facing African American men and women are clear: rising unemployment, mass incarceration, police harassment, and extra-judicial killings, now finally being caught on camera by regular people thanks to cell-phone technology. None of these issues is new, of course. But in a new century, the old narrative of American racism is being met by a revived civil rights movement, driven by expanding awareness and social media savvy, by groups like Black Lives Matter, and by politically conscious African Americans with a platform enabled by success—success that in itself was made possible by the voices and consciences of the many brave men and women who had spoken up in even more difficult times in the past.

Leading this movement of postmillennial sports figures with a political agenda has been LeBron James. While establishing himself as arguably the best player in the history of basketball, with three NBA championships added to his astonishing array of skills, James has become perhaps the most outspoken black athlete in the history of modern sports, willing to speak his mind on any topic that affects society as a whole, and the African American community in particular.

One of the best examples of James's leadership was in July 2016, when, supported by fellow NBA stars Carmelo Anthony, Chris Paul, and Dwyane Wade, he chose to use the platform of the ESPY Awards to demonstrate very public political leadership.

No one would call the ESPYs an overly serious affair. Akin to the Emmys and Oscars, these awards are light, comedic, and mostly for publicity. But leading up to the ceremony that July, it had been a tragic week for young African American men. The latest fatal police shootings—of Alton Sterling in Louisiana and Philando Castile in Minnesota—had extended a timeline of violence as old as the country and as far from solutions as ever. It was a week that LeBron and his fellow athlete-activists felt they could not ignore.

On stage that evening, Chris Paul stated the situation bluntly. The nephew of a police officer, he praised those public servants who serve American communities with conscience and integrity, but said, "Tray-von Martin. Michael Brown. Tamir Rice. Eric Garner. Laquan McDonald. Alton Sterling. Philando Castile. This is also our reality." Dwyane Wade added: "The racial profiling has to stop. The shoot-to-kill mentality has to stop. Not seeing the value of black and brown bodies has to stop." Standing in a row, dressed in black, these proud men were sending a physical as well as verbal message. *We are strong. We are together.* "The system is broken," Anthony said. "The problems are not new. The violence is not new. And the racial divide definitely is not new. But the urgency to create change is at an all-time high."

The sense that they were working from within a tradition of athlete activism was obvious. Paul put it this way: "Generations ago, legends like Jesse Owens, Jackie Robinson, Muhammad Ali, John Carlos and Tommie Smith, Kareem Abdul-Jabbar, Jim Brown, Billie Jean King, Arthur Ashe,

Since his rookie season with the NBA's Cleveland Cavaliers in 2003, LeBron James has been recognized as the greatest player in the current game, if not all time. He is also unafraid to call out bigotry when he sees it—even from the president of the United States.

and countless others, they set a model for what athletes should stand for. So we choose to follow in their footsteps." In other words: *We hold ourselves accountable.* And LeBron summed it up, stressing the onus of owning the responsibility of their fame and their race: "Let's use this moment as a call to action for all professional athletes to educate ourselves. It's for these issues. Speak up. Use our influence. And renounce all violence."

Was it a coincidence that, only a month or so after those awards, quarterback Colin Kaepernick chose to kneel during the national anthem before a preseason game between the San Francisco 49ers, Kaepernick's team, and the Green Bay Packers? The requirement to address the killings was in the air. The need for leadership was palpable. In the weeks following Kaepernick's controversial kneeling, James weighed in more informally: "For me, my personal feeling is that I got a twelve-year-old son, a nine-year-old son, and a two-year-old daughter, and I look at my son being four years removed from driving his own car and being able to leave the house on his own, and it's a scary thought right now to think if my son gets pulled over," he said. "You see these videos that continue to come out, and it's a scary-ass situation that if my son calls me and says that he's been pulled over that I'm not that confident that things are going to go well and my son is going to return home. And my son just started the sixth grade."

Those words, typical of James, are powerful and forthright. He is fully conscious of the depth and breadth of his influence. He is the face of the NBA, a man with international recognition. In 2017, he was listed by *Time* magazine as one of the world's 100 most influential people. He knows that there is no such thing as a casual comment, given the global reach of his personal brand. So he weighs what he says carefully. And his actions. Not long after his words at the ESPYs, James made a $2.5 million donation to the Smithsonian National Museum of African American History and Culture for an exhibit on Muhammad Ali. The following year, he joined with the school board in his hometown of Akron, Ohio, to create what his foundation called the I Promise School, a public elementary school aimed at at-risk children (James would later comment that it was the most important professional accomplishment of his life).

James has been active and outspoken from early in his professional career, weighing in substantively on issues such as the war in the Sudan, immigration, the Donald Sterling case, and the Unite the Right rally in Charlottesville, Virginia. He has been a consistent supporter of the Black Lives Matter movement and a champion of diversity and inclusion. His political vision has matured over time, as he developed the tact required of a man whose every public word is recorded and published.

When James spoke out at the ESPYs, he was supported by three contemporaries who share superstar talent, friendship, and a vision of social justice. Like James, Carmelo Anthony and Dwyane Wade were part of the outstanding 2003 NBA draft class (the first, third, and fifth picks, respectively). Chris Paul was the fourth pick in the 2005 draft. These young men were born decades after the civil rights movement of the sixties, and yet they all grew up in circumstances that, in different ways, provided lifelong reminders of the challenges African Americans still face.

Born in North Carolina, Paul was raised in a family that valued academics as much as athletics—their parents required that he and his brothers keep their grade point averages above 3.0 if they wanted to play high school sports. Paul's father, Charles, had attended a variety of schools in North Carolina because of forced busing; he and his wife, Robin, raised their children to be clear-eyed and open about race, and also to be guided by their religious principles. As one of the greatest point guards ever to play the game, Paul has shown natural leadership on the basketball court, but his off-court presence and political ability are such that in 2013, he was elected president of the NBA Players Association.

At that point in his career, Paul was playing for the Los Angeles Clippers. He supported Clippers head coach Doc Rivers and NBA commissioner Adam Silver when the league banned Sterling from the NBA for life

Doc Rivers was never afraid to back down—as point guard for the Atlanta Hawks, coach for a number of NBA teams, or when teenagers broke into his family home and burned it down in 1997.

and forced him to sell the team for making his virulent racist remarks. It was a bold, unprecedented move; owners have the money, and money gives power, even over superstar athletes. But Paul was judicious and wise in his handling of the situation and in countering this financial power with the moral power of informed leadership, discussing at one point the possibility of a boycott if Sterling did not sell the team.

Carmelo Anthony had an upbringing fraught with danger, first in the housing developments of Brooklyn and then in Baltimore, where his mother worked as a housekeeper and the family survived on food stamps. At fourteen, he was robbed at gunpoint for twenty dollars. His neighborhood was known as "the Pharmacy" because of its wide availability of drugs. "I could have gone that way," Anthony said. "Some friends did. But I started seeing that by playing basketball, I could make more money than they did. When you've never had something, you want it worse than anything."

Anthony is proud of his country. A member of the USA Olympic basketball team a record four times, from 2004 to 2016, he has won a bronze and three gold medals and is the national basketball team's all-time leading scorer, rebounder, and leader in games played. But he has been unafraid to challenge his country's political leadership when he sees it failing to address injustice. After Donald Trump's presidential election in 2016, Anthony—then playing for the New York Knicks in the media capital of the United States—was crestfallen. Surrounded by a horde of reporters after a game, he stood in front of his locker and spoke at length about his

FAMILY ACTIVISM

WHEN THE RACIST REMARKS of Los Angeles Clippers owner Donald Sterling went public, Clippers head coach Doc Rivers stepped up quickly to work with Chris Paul, NBA commissioner Adam Silver, and others to get Sterling banned from the NBA. It wasn't the first time that Rivers, a former All-Star point guard and veteran NBA coach, was forced to confront racism. When Rivers was a college player at Marquette University in the early 1980s, during his freshman year, he met and fell in love with his future wife, Kris Campion, who is white. They were both stunned when the tires on Kris's car were slashed and a racial epithet was scrawled on the sidewalk in front of her parents' house. The strength of their relationship and the support of Rivers's coach at the time helped them deal with the bigotry. They would need that strength years later, when their family home in San Antonio was burned down under suspicious circumstances. The Sterling incident would bring all that back to the family. As Rivers's son, Jeremiah, remembered in a series of tweets, "Along with anything we ever loved and held treasured, because of the color of my dad's skin, we lost everything and had to start over." But Jeremiah had learned well from his dad and mom. As he also tweeted, "Racism isn't born, it's taught. It is the refuge of ignorance and seeks to divide and destroy."

disappointment, concluding with the words: "I just don't know what I'm going to tell my son. We need to find a way to go on."

Anthony remembers what it was like growing up in the streets that inspired the HBO series *The Wire*. He knows that addressing the challenges of that environment will take education, enlightened policy, sympathy, and support, from family to community to government. He recognizes his luck in escaping the worst of growing up in an impoverished, violent location, and that his mother's support was critical. Mary Anthony, or "Miss Mary" as she was known, worked two low-paying jobs to raise her four children and taught them the importance of education and respect for others. "It was tough," she has said, "but it was something I had to do. By the grace of God, I made it through. I just did what came natural." Carmelo's response? "I take my hat off to her. There's nothing I can do in my lifetime to pay her back."

Like Paul, Dwyane Wade has a strong value system based on his experience in the church. But like Anthony, Wade's early life was also harsh and dangerous, a product of the roughest of the rough streets of Chicago's South Side. Wade himself has spoken of his tough background—that his mother used and dealt drugs, that his family grew up in a gang environment, that as a child, he saw needles lying around and came across dead bodies. Police raids were a fact of life. "When you speak about Dwyane and his commitment to preventing shootings in the community," the broadcaster Jason Jackson has said, "you're speaking of a man who as a kid dodged actual bullets there. He knows he has to help. Because he was nearly shot down himself."

Wade would be reminded of the reality of violence and the dangers of being young and black many times, including in 2012, when he was a member of the Miami Heat along with LeBron James—the team that would win back-to-back championships in 2012 and 2013. On February 26, 2012, the same night that the NBA All-Star Game was being played, a black teenager named Trayvon Martin was killed by George Zimmerman, a neighborhood watch coordinator of a gated community in Sanford, Florida. Martin was returning home from a convenience store and was carrying only an iced tea and a bag of Skittles. But he was wearing a hoodie—a fact that sparked a national debate about racial profiling.

Sanford is just a few hours from Miami, and the incident had a real impact on the Heat. Wade posted a photo of himself on Twitter and Facebook wearing a hoodie. A few days later, James posted a photo of the Heat players, taken at their team hotel, all wearing hoodies, heads bowed, hands in their pockets. One of the hashtags: #WeWantJustice.

Although profiled killings of young, unarmed black men and women, by police officers and others, are nothing new, the spate of incidents in the years following the Trayvon Martin case sparked a nationwide response. The deaths were frequent and similar in pattern. In 2014 alone: Eric Garner in July. Michael Brown and Ezell Ford in August. Laquan McDonald in October. Akai Gurley, twelve-year-old Tamir Rice, and John Crawford in November. All killed by police. All unarmed. Some were shot in the back. The deaths continued, as communities mounted protests nationwide. And they continue to the present day. The ESPYs moment must be viewed in this context.

These are the men who challenged their league, their fans, and their fellow athletes at the ESPYs. As Wade put it, "We just felt our voices needed to be heard. We used the platform that we had. It was the biggest night that sports has. As leaders of the NBA, we decided we should take this moment, before the show started, before the celebration, before we talk about awards. . . . As much as anything, we wanted to speak to the *other* athletes. To tell them that *their* voices needed to be heard. And also: there are others who are making changes and contributions and they hadn't been recognized, and needed to be encouraged to keep doing it."

Since that night, Wade has continued to focus on the campaign to address gun violence in all its forms. In February 2018, after spells with the Chicago Bulls and Cleveland Cavaliers, he was traded back to the Miami Heat. In a sense, he was coming home. This was where he had won his three championship rings. A week after his return, seventeen high school students were killed in a mass shooting in Parkland, Florida. Wade acted immediately, speaking out on social media, visiting Marjory Stoneman Douglas High School unannounced, and donating $200,000 to the March for Our Lives, a student-led march against gun violence. He also dedicated the rest of his season to one of the victims, Joaquin Oliver, who had been buried wearing a Wade jersey. "I can't imagine what these families are dealing with," Wade said, "what they are going through. But what I try to do is I try to put myself in that situation and the heartache and the hurt, just even trying to imagine it, is too much to bear."

Wade, Anthony, and Paul are examples of how African American athlete activism has matured in the age of social media and Black Lives Matter. The NBA—the major US sports league with the highest percentage of black players—has itself shown maturity and leadership, and the career of LeBron James is perhaps the crowning example of its willingness to engage with the world outside of athletic competition.

James has been in the spotlight since the days when he was a phenomenon at St. Vincent–St. Mary High School in Akron, Ohio, where he became the first sophomore to be named to *USA TODAY*'s All-USA First Team. But the road to that level of national attention was not easy. He grew up in a fatherless household, and his mother, Gloria, struggled to support her family, especially after her grandmother and mother passed away within a year of each other. Their stability lost, Gloria and her young son led a virtually homeless life in Akron, moving twelve times. "That's when things really got tough," James has said. "It was a mess. It was survival. There was violence. I saw so much I wouldn't want my kids to see."

As an eight-year-old, James missed 100 out of 162 days of school. Around that time, desperately trying to avoid a life of crime herself, Gloria gave in and asked one of her son's youth coaches, Frank Walker, to take LeBron in. James would never forget the way that Walker and his family opened up his home to him and his mom. "Growing up in the inner city," James later said, "the statistics were always stacked up against you. What happened with me is that around the fourth grade, I got some mentors and teachers and some Little League coaches that I started to believe in. And they started to make me believe my dreams could become a reality."

And basketball also rescued him. Or, more precisely, his unparalleled skill and ferocious work ethic did. He was a true prodigy, so dominant in high school that an NBA career was a lock. He was drafted first overall by the Cleveland Cavaliers in 2003, directly out of high school, and he created a sea change in the league. He could control all five positions on the basketball court. He was dominant from the first NBA game he played, when he scored 25 points against the Sacramento Kings. His amazing skills, his killer instinct, and his vision instantly made the Cavaliers a force to be reckoned with. He was eighteen years old.

This teenager had guidance: Gloria was always on the scene, as well as mentors such as NBA legend Paul Silas, his first NBA head coach. Silas taught him to listen to the positive and to ignore players who resented his innate skills and intelligence. Like Chris Paul, Silas had been a president of the NBA Players Association, a man who combined a fearsome basketball presence with plenty of political shrewdness. He was ideal for the young James, helping him on and off the court.

James played for Cleveland for seven seasons; departed for Miami, where, alongside Wade and Chris Bosh, he led the Heat to back-to-back NBA championships; and then returned to Cleveland for another four years, when he led the Cavaliers to four consecutive Eastern Conference titles and, in 2016, the city's first NBA championship. From Cleveland, he moved on to the Los Angeles Lakers, brought on board by then club president Magic Johnson in an effort to bring the Lakers franchise back to its glory days. But wherever he has played, James has never abandoned his roots. He has invested tens of millions of dollars in northeast Ohio and has built a formidable economic empire with a group of friends from Akron.

His legacy is unquestioned. As early as 2008, NBA coach Mike Brown said, "Before he's finished playing, LeBron will go down as the greatest player of all time." The debate over the Greatest of All Time (GOAT) in basketball will never end, and there are plenty of worthy candidates to consider, from Bill Russell to Larry Bird to Michael Jordan. But James's activism and outspokenness, his fame beyond basketball, and his leadership must be added to his athletic greatness when we are considering what he has done both for his sport and for social justice causes.

The men who run the NFL and own its teams could learn much from the NBA. The basketball league, for the most part, treats its activist athletes with respect and acknowledges the history of activism. Before the 2018 All-Star Game, held in Los Angeles, NBA commissioner Adam Silver made a point of honoring Bill Russell, who was sitting in the front row as Silver held a press conference ahead of the midseason festivities. Silver noted that, fifty-five years earlier, the 1963 All-Star Game had also been held in Los Angeles, and in that game, Russell had led the East to victory with twenty-four rebounds and an all-round performance that earned him the game's MVP award. But, Silver pointed out, 1963 was also the year that Russell attended the Great March on Washington, listening closely as Dr. King made his historic "I Have a Dream" speech. Russell was creating his own historical record, as the best basketball player in the world and as a black man of pride and conscience.

Today's NBA players stand on the shoulders of Russell and others who walked before them. And the 2016 ESPYs should be seen as a starting point for an enhanced and more engaged activism. Americans love their sports. Let us understand that sports happens not in a vacuum, but in the context of a political culture. Let us follow LeBron when he says, as he did on that night, "We all feel helpless and frustrated by the violence. We do. But that's not acceptable. It's time to look in the mirror and ask ourselves, what are we doing to create change? It's not about being a role model. It's not about our responsibility to the tradition of activism. . . . We all have to do better."

TAKING A KNEE
Colin Kaepernick

12

ON SEPTEMBER 1, 2016, eighty years after Jesse Owens's four-gold-medal performance at the Berlin Olympics, Colin Kaepernick first knelt in protest during the national anthem and ignited the latest firestorm over an African American athlete's right to protest. Much of the controversy has been a misunderstanding—and a willful one in many cases. And much of it is unfair. Kaepernick has stated that he was not criticizing American veterans or disrespecting his country in his action. Just the opposite: in exercising his First Amendment right to free speech, he was making a powerful statement about how—after a century of progressive black athlete activism—the country he loves was still mired in attitudes and actions that perpetuated racism and undermined the high ideals of its citizens and its constitution. It was, in fact, a highly patriotic gesture.

His activism was instantly dissected on social media. There were those who supported him, including veterans who spoke out about his right to protest (trending with the hashtag #VeteransforKaepernick).

Mahmoud Abdul-Rauf, the NBA player who had courted controversy twenty years earlier with a similar protest, said that Kaepernick had "a lot to lose" and demonstrated bravery and selflessness by being "willing to put all of that on the line because, to him, truth is more important."

Barack Obama, who was president then, also weighed in. "I'd rather have young people who are engaged in the argument," he said, "and trying to think through how they can be part of our democratic process than people who are sitting on the sidelines not paying attention at all."

But there was also the inevitable backlash, some of it reasonably expressed, but much of it not: A Twitter storm of invective. Hate mail. Death threats. And then a new president, whose false narrative and unthinking, vitriolic rhetoric on this subject encouraged the likeminded to create an atmosphere of hostility toward Kaepernick, both inside and outside the NFL. This was the same president, Donald Trump, who, not long afterward, said that there were "very fine people on both sides" of a confrontation that took place during the "Unite the Right" rally in Charlottesville, Virginia, between neofascist marchers, who carried Nazi and neo-Nazi symbols while chanting racist and anti-Semitic slogans, and protestors aghast at the ugly and obvious attempt to assert white supremacy. He was drawing a specious equivalence between the oppressors and those who sought to resist them.

In this divided world, Kaepernick's actions were bound to have contradictory consequences. As an activist, he has been honored—by Amnesty International, the American Civil Liberties Union, and many other organizations that care about civil rights. And support has also come from at least one global business. In 2018, he was revealed as a new face of Nike's "Just Do It" campaign, which featured a black-and-white close-up of Kaepernick's visage with the superimposed words, "Believe in something. Even if it means sacrificing everything. Just do it." Serena Williams and LeBron James, both part of the campaign, praised Nike. Others responded with fury, threatening to boycott the brand.

As a professional football player, however, Kaepernick's fortunes had taken a dramatic reverse. Three years before his protest, after starting the season on the sidelines, he had led the San Francisco 49ers to the Super Bowl and, at the ESPYs that year, received the Best Breakthrough Athlete award. Following his preseason kneel, he had an up-and-down season with the 49ers, and in March 2017, he opted out of his contract and became a free agent. But this twenty-nine-year-old man, a starting quarterback still in his athletic prime who had thrown sixteen touchdown passes in eleven games, couldn't even land a backup role. To date, he hasn't played a minute in the NFL since, and his suit against the NFL for collusion was finally settled with a large cash payout by the league that can be seen as a de facto admission of guilt. It is hoped that the settlement will also encourage a team to give him a contract and allow him to continue in his profession.

Kaepernick (and his 49ers teammate Eric Reid, who knelt beside him) were not the first to use the national anthem as a platform for protest, of course, and their taking a knee was just the latest statement in a dialogue that many in the NFL, as throughout society, had been having since the death of Trayvon Martin and the rise of Black Lives Matter. Often, the debate has been spirited. In 2015, Seattle Seahawks cornerback Richard Sherman questioned the rhetoric of Black Lives Matter and was challenged in a press conference the next day by teammate Michael Bennett. Bennett, who would later be thrown to the ground and handcuffed by Las Vegas police in a case of what he insisted was racial profiling, has been a significant voice—an active player's voice—in twenty-first-century athlete activism. And there have been other NFL voices: Anquan Boldin, Doug Baldwin, Devin McCourty, and Malcolm Jenkins have all been at the forefront of efforts to encourage a healthy questioning of what their league and their society are doing about social justice.

It is a complicated dialogue. Since the terrorist attacks of September 11, 2001, sporting events have been given a military dimension, featuring honor guards, giant flags, and promotions paid for by the various branches of the armed services. These trappings have led many fans to see any protest as being antiveteran. But Kaepernick, Bennett, Jenkins, and other African American protesters have been very clear that their actions have nothing to do with the military. Their voices are part of a wider cultural movement, a reaction to a series of tragedies that has sometimes been visceral, sometimes thoughtful; sometimes violent, usually controlled. They do not want the country to forget the extrajudicial killings of young black men, which have pushed race to the forefront of consciousness and directed a magnifying glass on related issues: the militarization of American police departments, the demographic disparities between many police forces and their citizenry, and deep racial and political divisions in the reactions to the shootings and their aftermaths.

Their voices also remind us that the NFL presents a unique challenge, which makes it the focal point for African American athletes seeking to draw attention to racism. Unlike the administrative structure of the NBA, which has, on the whole, a recent record of informed and sympathetic engagement with its players' activism, the ownership and executives running the NFL have mixed narratives in response to protests by their players. Kaepernick's inability to get a contract with any NFL team speaks for itself, of course. And while some league owners have been measured and fair-minded in their reaction, many simply see protest as being bad for business (the NFL is the largest single entertainment property in the United States and distributes more than $8 billion in revenue to its thirty-two teams). Money talks. And unfortunately, what it usually says is: "Shut up and play. Keep politics out of it." As if the owners, and the head coaches who are often their mouthpieces, are not political in their attempts to shape the narrative and silence protest.

NFL star and Super Bowl champion Michael Bennett's voice has been clear in response. In many ways, he has taken up the NFL leadership role from Kaepernick. In 2018, he published a memoir, *Things That Make White*

Michael Bennett (left) and Colin Kaepernick speak after a 2016 NFL game between the Seattle Seahawks and the San Francisco 49ers. Bennett has been an outspoken supporter of Kaepernick and a committed advocate for social change.

People Uncomfortable, which takes a thorough look at the current athlete activism agenda and makes forceful, honest statements about the mixed narratives about it. He refuses to be silenced. "There are teams whose head coaches even try to get players to sign a code of conduct, promising not to bring politics into the locker room," he has written. It's a way of "trying to keep people in a box. It's also insulting: telling a group of grown-ass men basically not to talk to each other."

In his book, Bennett acknowledges Kaepernick's key role. "Colin opened up so many eyes and took so much abuse for stepping out first. It hurt him that he is a quarterback, the face of a franchise. He was also at the end of his contract. The courage to do what he did, given his situation, is greatly undervalued." But Bennett also understands that the dialogue within the NFL must move beyond the controversy of a single issue. The problems needing to be addressed are wide-ranging: getting the league to commit funds to social-justice causes, alleviating poverty, improving education, combating violence against women, and making sure that the food we eat and the environment we live in are safe. "We are living in a defining moment," Bennett writes. "We are at a crossroads when it comes to our youth, their lives, the food they eat, the air they breathe, and the kind of lives they are going to lead."

Other players have helped move the dialogue to a broader level. Malcolm Jenkins, a teammate when Bennett later played for the Philadelphia Eagles, cofounded the Players Coalition, an organization aimed at bringing together disparate athlete activist efforts and focusing them on justice reform, in Philadelphia and elsewhere. Coalition members, including cofounder Anquan Boldin and New England Patriots safety Devin McCourty, have visited prisons and met continually with police departments, public defenders, and lawmakers. They have also sat down with NFL owners, imploring them to funnel significant economic investment into the community.

Jenkins, who had raised a fist during the national anthem in a preseason game himself, has led the coalition's efforts to secure an $89 million commitment from the NFL toward the cause of racial justice. He is proof of Bennett's belief that making people uncomfortable—especially white people—is an important step in the road to social change. But Jenkins also shows how important it is for these athletes to make *themselves* uncomfortable. Just as LeBron demanded, he is looking in the mirror and asking what he can do to create change.

Jenkins has acknowledged the intersectionality of their fight and given Bennett a shout-out for his widening of the conversation about race. Bennett "brings up ideas that have been a little outside of our scope," he has said. "He'll bring up women's rights, he's big on sustainable food . . . things like that." For his part, Bennett has argued that "it's important to say we want black freedom, but we can't say we want these different things if we don't respect women." This comment is especially important in the context of several high-profile cases of spousal abuse by NFL players. The cult of "manhood" that was part of Jim Brown's self-image remains a danger-

Chris Long (left) supports his teammate Malcolm Jenkins with a hand on his back while Jenkins and Rodney McLeod (number 23) raise their fists during the national anthem before a 2017 NFL game between the Philadelphia Eagles and Chicago Bears.

ous myth among football players, leading to anger becoming a false virtue. And it doesn't help when owners and the NFL authorities themselves are more forgiving of abuse of women than they are of anthem protests.

And so the tradition continues. Kaepernick's high-profile protest has drawn attention to a broader and continually developing movement that reaches into the past while it looks to the future. Sometimes the links are literal—as when Bennett became friends with John Carlos through Athletes for Impact, an organization that connects athletes with communities to "positively transform America." Other times, it is symbolic—Jenkins, Bennett, and other current activists are inspired by those who have gone before them. But in all cases, the awareness and action of these twenty-first-century activists are aimed at *keeping the conversation going*.

As Jenkins has put it, "I want there to be no excuse but to deal with these things in a real way. And so, while we may move away from demonstrations during the national anthem, there's going to be a lot of things to come that make sure our voices are heard and make sure that we keep things loud and clear and in the front of people's minds. . . . At the end of the day, whether there are people praising you or the President criticizing you, it keeps the conversation in the forefront."

EPILOGUE

NO ONE FIGHTS ALONE. Colin Kaepernick and Malcolm Jenkins, Michael Bennett and LeBron James, Venus and Serena Williams— all these athletes pursue excellence in their sports, while remembering the sacrifices made by those who came before them. They extend the lines of influence defined by Jackie Robinson and Wilma Rudolph. By Bill Russell and Arthur Ashe. By Muhammad Ali and Kareem Abdul-Jabbar. The cultural circumstances change as the years pass, but the issues are the same and the stakes remain high. To paraphrase Russell yet again, you only register progress by how far you have to go, not how far you've come.

The story goes on. In 2019, Super Bowl LIII was held in Atlanta, the hometown of Dr. King; it was early February—Black History Month. Eager to create an atmosphere of respect and acknowledgment of King's legacy, the NFL invited King's youngest daughter, Dr. Bernice A. King, to oversee the coin toss before the game. She was joined by Andrew Young and John Lewis, two icons of the civil rights movement in politics. But even the presence of these African American heroes was not enough to quell controversy. Supporters of Colin Kaepernick said that, at best, the invitations were a public relations exercise by the NFL, and they noted the absence of any meaningful progress with the collusion grievance that Kaepernick had filed against the NFL in 2017.

Then, just days after the Super Bowl, the announcement came that the league *would* settle the grievance (and a second grievance filed by Kaepernick's fellow protestor, Eric Reid, in 2018) for a reported $10 million. The first grievance had accused the NFL and its owners of colluding to "deprive Mr. Kaepernick of employment rights in retaliation for Mr. Kaepernick's leadership and advocacy for equality and social justice and his bringing awareness to peculiar institutions still undermining racial equality in the United States." The settlements opened the opportunity for Kaepernick and Reid to resume playing football and—many hope—may lead to support for a more tolerant atmosphere for thoughtful protest at NFL games and other sports events.

But the reality remains that, as Kareem Abdul-Jabbar put it, the NFL's "moral convictions are bottom-line based." And Abdul-Jabbar's view is an important one here. His is perhaps the most important current voice in African American athlete activism, and he brings the wisdom and experience of his long life in sports and politics to his judgments. He argues that the NFL settled the grievances with Kaepernick and Reid because that was the most expedient way of getting the issue off the table. He believes that we do not direct as much scrutiny on leagues and owners as we do on players. As he has written,

> Sports is a major symbol of American values of fair play, sportsmanship, dedication, sacrifice, discipline, and teamwork. In many parts of the Midwest and the South, high school football is America. But the NFL is putting all that in jeopardy when it refuses to take a leadership role in standing up for the Constitution—and the rights of athletes like Reid

and Kaepernick to protest peacefully—instead of cowering in the ticket booth counting money, afraid to offend people who place entertainment over ethics.

Perhaps it is hoping for too much that a league with the power and money that the NFL has will do the right thing, even when it means angering some of its fans or potentially losing revenue. But more broadly, Kaepernick's kneeling—and the pressure that Abdul-Jabbar and others continue to put on our culture—are examples of the kind of leadership that must be shown consistently if progress is to continue to be made. As Abdul-Jabbar reminds us, this is what progress comes down to. Leadership.

So, yes, the story continues. Leadership inspires others to lead. In the summer of 2019, Kaepernick, according to the *Wall Street Journal*, requested that Nike cancel plans to release a shoe featuring an "Old Glory" flag because of its associations with a period in American history marked by slavery and the fact that that version of the flag has sometimes been adopted and displayed by white supremacist groups. Also that summer, one of the stars of the World Cup-winning US women's soccer team, Megan Rapinoe, who is gay, joined Kaepernick's protest by kneeling during the national anthem ahead of US World Cup matches. "I haven't experienced over-policing, racial profiling, police brutality or the sight of a family member's body lying dead in the street," she wrote of her decision. "But I cannot stand idly by while there are people in this country who have had to deal with that kind of heartache." After President Trump publicly criticized her for her stand, she declared in strong terms that she would not visit the White House if the team were invited.

This book has told the stories of some of the greatest American leaders of the last 100 years—in sports and in life—women and men who have had the courage to make the sacrifice that leadership demands. Because true leadership means putting the concerns of the group ahead of the achievements of the individual, the commitment and selflessness of these athletes outside their sporting lives will, in the march of history, be seen as being far more significant than any personal bests or championship rings.

Kyle Korver, a white NBA player who recognizes his privilege, has written: "The fact that inequality is built so deeply into so many of our most trusted institutions is wrong. And I believe it's the responsibility of anyone on the privileged end of those inequalities to help make things right." He knows that leadership must come from all communities. Leadership works on many levels. As citizens, every American, no matter what the race, has an opportunity to exercise the kind of personal initiative that leads to change. High-level leadership works only if it is followed by collective action—and collective action depends on enough of us, as ordinary readers, ordinary fans, and fellow Americans, responding to the call and demanding justice and equality in whatever way we can.

We can all take a knee. We can all call out unfairness and show courage. In this way, we can join the great athletes whose stories are told in this book, challenging injustice, taking a stand, helping to further the cause of justice and to subvert the poison of racism in their times and ours, and build a platform for future generations to continue the fight.

ACKNOWLEDGMENTS

TOO MANY PEOPLE TO THANK. Having been blessed to have been a part of the predominantly African American National Basketball Association community for over forty years, I believed it would be relatively easy to communicate about race and social justice. It was not. It's one thing to discuss The Game. It's entirely another to listen to the voices of those who have to deal with racism every day and to write about their challenges in a way that respects that I have not been where they have.

So the dialogues with my friends about the injustice of racism have given this book what insights it may offer. My first acknowledgment goes to Devin McCourty, who demonstrates how vital it is to take a stand. To Mike Conley and Bob Costas, whose support has been invaluable. To Thabo Sefalosha, who suffered an unjust, life-threatening assault by police and refused to be embittered by it while simultaneously seeking justice—and who willingly spoke to us. To Sean Elliott, who supported the need for this writer to continually examine internal presuppositions about race.

To my mentor at Ohio State, the late Dr. Harold Pepinsky. And to many others who gave me the benefit of their wisdom and experience: Samuel Freedman, Kyle Lowry, DeMar DeRozan, Cedric Maxwell, Kyle Draper, M. L. Carr, Bob Ryan, Nate Archibald, Robert Parish, Tom Heinsohn, Chris Webber, Quinn Buckner, Reggie Williams, Johnette Howard, Doris Burke, Steven Schron, Marilyn Likosky, Dr. William Likosky, Harvey Araton, Charles Scott, Jim Fenton, Isiah Thomas, Ron Borges, James Satch Sullinger, Jeff Twiss, Matt Zeysing, Bill Walton, and Larry Bird. And my friend LeBron James, whose commitment to his home in Northeast Ohio, creating the I Promise School and supporting the region with significant philanthropy, is an inspiration to all.

Other conversations, over time, helped my perspective. Coach Glenn "Doc" Rivers, in awe of Bill Russell, told me how amazed he was that Russell was able to become the Greatest of All Time while combating severe personal racial prejudice and becoming a leader of the movement. The proud, brilliant Bob Gibson inspired me with his words as well as his achievements on and off the field. And I am indebted to Oscar Robertson who, many years ago, made me conscious of how the descendants of slaves should be awarded reparations to compensate for the continued effects of slavery and Jim Crow.

To my editor at Imagine Publishing, Kevin Stevens, whose support, vision, leadership, and equanimity made this project possible. This was a collaborative effort in every sense. Our mantra was twofold: *strive for quality* and *get the message out*. And to the great team at Charlesbridge/Imagine, especially publisher Mary Ann Sabia and editor Karen Boss, who supported this book from the beginning and whose advice made it so much better.

To my wife, Edna, my daughter Laura and her husband, Kris, and my daughter Sarah and her husband, Kyle. The foundations.

PHOTO CREDITS

Kareem Abdul-Jabbar speaking on page 93: The Star-Ledger/The Image Works Inc.

Althea Gibson in action on page 97: International Tennis Hall of Fame

Althea Gibson descending from plane on page 98: International Tennis Hall of Fame/Pan Am

Arthur Ashe on pages 101 and 105: International Tennis Hall of Fame

Serena and Venus Williams on page 111 and Jackie Joyner-Kersee on page 121: TopPhoto/The Image Works Inc.

Jason Collins on page 125, Michael Jordan on page 131, Craig Hodges on page 136, Magic Johnson on page 139, and Doc Rivers on page 148: Steve Lipofsky/basketballphoto.com

Tiger Woods and three presidents on page 134 and LeBron James on page 145: The Star-Ledger/The Image Works Inc.

Michael Bennett and Colin Kaepernick on page 159: AP Photo/Ted S. Warren

Chris Long, Malcolm Jenkins, and Rodney McLeod on page 161: AP photo/Chris Szagola

SOURCES/FURTHER READING

THE FOLLOWING BOOKS, articles, and interviews have provided invaluable context, quotations, and detail for the writing of the stories and arguments in *Taking a Knee, Taking a Stand*. These pieces are excellent resources for readers who wish to explore the lives of these athletes in fuller detail or to delve more deeply into the history and politics of African American athlete activism.

Books

Abdul-Jabbar, Kareem. *Coach Wooden and Me: Our 50-Year Friendship on and off the Court.* New York: Hachette Books, 2017.

Abdul-Jabbar, Kareem, and Peter Knobler. *Giant Steps.* New York: Bantam, 1983.

Abdul-Jabbar, Kareem, and Mignon McCarthy. *Kareem.* New York: Random House, 1990.

Abdul-Jabbar, Kareem, and Raymond Obstfeld. *Writings on the Wall: Searching for a New Equality Beyond Black and White.* New York: Time Books, 2016.

Ali, Muhammad, and Richard Durham. *The Greatest: My Own Story.* New York: Random House, 1975.

Ambrose, Stephen. *To America: Personal Reflections of an Historian.* New York: Simon and Schuster, 2002.

Arsenault, Raymond. *Arthur Ashe: A Life.* New York: Simon & Schuster, 2018.

Ashe, Arthur. *A Hard Road to Glory: A History of the African-American Athlete, 1619–1990.* 3 vols. New York: Amistad, 1993.

Ashe, Arthur, and Arnold Rampersad. *Days of Grace: A Memoir.* New York: Ballantine, 1993.

Baldwin, James. *The Fire Next Time.* New York: Random House, 1963.

Barkley, Charles, and Michael Wilbon. *I May Be Wrong but I Doubt It.* New York: Random House, 2005.

Benedict, Jeff, and Armen Keteyian. *Tiger Woods.* New York: Simon and Schuster, 2018.

Bennett, Michael, and Dave Zirin. *Things That Make White People Uncomfortable.* Chicago: Haymarket Books, 2018.

Branch, Taylor. *Parting the Waters: America in the King Years, 1954–63.* New York: Simon & Schuster, 1988.

Brown, Jim, and Steve Delsohn. *Jim Brown: Out of Bounds.* New York: Kensington Books, 1989.

Dweck, Carol. *Mindset: The New Psychology of Success.* New York: Random House, 2006.

Early, Gerald. *A Level Playing Field: African American Athletes and the Republic of Sports.* Boston: Harvard University Press, 2011.

Edwards, Harry. *The Revolt of the Black Athlete: 50th Anniversary Edition.* Urbana: University of Illinois Press, 2017.

Freeman, Mike. *Jim Brown: The Fierce Life of an American Hero.* New York: William Morrow, 2006.

Gates, Henry Louis, Jr., and Cornel West. *The African-American Century: How Black Americans Have Shaped Our Country.* New York: Free Press, 2000.

Goodwin, Doris Kearns. *Leadership in Turbulent Times.* New York: Simon & Schuster, 2018.

Goudsouzian, Aram. *King of the Court: Bill Russell and the Basketball Revolution.* Berkeley: University of California Press, 2010.

Gray, Frances Clayton, and Yanick Rice Lamb. *Born to Win: The Authorized Biography of Althea Gibson.* Hoboken, NJ: Wiley, 2004.

Halberstam, David. *Playing for Keeps: Michael Jordan and the World He Made.* New York: Random House, 2000.

Halberstam, David. *October 1964.* New York: Ballantine Reprint, 1995.

Hauser, Thomas. *Muhammad Ali: His Life and Times*. New York: Simon & Schuster, 1991.

Hawkins, Billy. *The New Plantation: Black Athletes, College Sports, and Predominantly White NCAA Institutions*. New York: Palgrave, 2010.

Hoffer, Richard. *Something in the Air: American Passion and Defiance in the 1968 Mexico City Olympics*. New York: Free Press, 2009.

Johnson, Earvin "Magic," and William Novak. *My Life*. New York: Random House, 1992.

Joyner-Kersee, Jackie, and Sonja Steptoe. *A Kind of Grace: The Autobiography of the World's Greatest Female Athlete*. New York: Time Warner, 1997.

Kahn, Roger. *Rickey and Robinson: The True, Untold Story of the Integration of Baseball*. New York: Rodale, 2014.

King, Billie Jean, and Christine Brennan. *Pressure Is a Privilege: Lessons I've Learned from Life and the Battle of the Sexes*. New York: LifeTime Media, 2008.

Koehn, Nancy. *Forged in Crisis: The Power of Courageous Leadership in Turbulent Times*. New York: Simon & Schuster, 2017.

Lloyd, Jason. *The Blueprint: LeBron James, Cleveland's Deliverance, and the Making of the Modern NBA*. New York: Dutton, 2017.

Mandela, Nelson. *Mandela: An Illustrated Autobiography*. Boston: Little Brown, 1996.

Maraniss, David. *Rome 1960: The Olympics That Changed the World*. New York: Simon & Schuster, 2008.

Margolick, David. *Beyond Glory: Joe Louis vs. Max Schmeling and a World on the Brink*. New York: Random House, 2006.

Marqusee, Mike. *Redemption Song: Muhammad Ali and the Spirit of the Sixties*. London and New York: Verso, 2016.

McRae, Donald. *Heroes Without a Country, America's Betrayal of Joe Louis and Jesse Owens*. New York: Ecco, 2003.

Montville, Leigh. *Sting Like a Bee: Muhammad Ali Versus the United States of America 1966–1971*. New York: Doubleday, 2017.

Obama, Barack. *Dreams from My Father: A Story of Race and Inheritance*. New York: Crown Reprint, 2007.

Rampersad, Arnold. *Jackie Robinson: A Biography*. New York: Knopf, 1997.

Remnick, David. *King of the World: Muhammad Ali and the Rise of an American Hero*. New York: Random House, 1998.

Roberts, Randy. *Joe Louis: Hard Times Man*. New Haven: Yale University Press, 2010.

Roberts, Randy, and Johnny Smith. *Blood Brothers: The Fatal Friendship Between Muhammad Ali and Malcolm X*. New York: Basic Books, 2016.

Roberts, Selena. *A Necessary Spectacle: Billie Jean King, Bobby Riggs, and the Tennis Match That Leveled the Game*. New York: Crown, 2005.

Robertson, Oscar. *The Big O: My Life, My Times, My Game*. New York: Rodale, 2003.

Robinson, Jackie, and Alfred Duckett. *I Never Had It Made: An Autobiography*. New York: Ecco, 1995.

Russell, Bill, and Taylor Branch. *Second Wind*. New York: Random House, 1979.

Russell, Bill, and David Falkner. *Russell Rules: 11 Lessons on Leadership from the Twentieth Century's Greatest Winner*. New York: Dutton, 2001.

Russell, Bill, and Alan Steinberg. *Red and Me*. New York: HarperCollins, 2009.

Schaap, Jeremy. *Triumph: The Untold Story of Jesse Owens and Hitler's Olympics*. Boston: Houghton Mifflin Harcourt, 2007.

Schron, Bob, and Kevin Stevens. *The Bird Era*. Boston: Quinlan Press, 1989.

Smith, Maureen Margaret. *Wilma Rudolph: A Biography*. Westport, CT: Greenwood Press, 2006.

Smith, Tommie. *Silent Gesture: The Autobiography of Tommie Smith*. Philadelphia: Temple University Press, 2007.

Tygiel, Jules. *Baseball's Great Experiment: Jackie Robinson and His Legacy*. Oxford, UK, and New York: Oxford University Press, 2008.

Williams, Richard, and Bart Davis. *Black and White: The Way I See It*. New York: Simon & Schuster, 2014.

Windhorst, Brian, and Dave McMenamin. *Return of the King: LeBron James, the Cleveland Cavaliers and the Greatest Comeback in NBA History*. New York: Hachette, 2017.

Zirin, Dave. *Jim Brown: Last Man Standing*. New York: Blue Rider Press, 2018.

Zirin, Dave. *The John Carlos Story: The Sports Moment That Changed the World*. Chicago: Haymarket Books, 2011.

Zirin, Dave. *What's My Name, Fool? Sports and Resistance in the United States*. Chicago: Haymarket Books, 2005.

Articles

Abdul-Jabbar, Kareem. "College Athletes of the World, Unite." *Jacobin*, November 12, 2014.

Abdul-Jabbar, Kareem. "The NFL's Settlement with Kaepernick Should Just Be the Start of Making Amends." *The Guardian*, February 16, 2019.

Abdul-Jabbar, Kareem. "Why I have Mixed Feelings about MLK Day." *Time*, January 18, 2015.

Anderson, Dave. "Sports of the Times: On Loyalty to Company, or Country?" *New York Times*, August 2, 1992.

Bagchi, Rob. "50 Stunning Olympic Moments No. 35: Wilma Rudolph's Triple Gold in 1960." *The Guardian*, June 1, 2012.

Belson, Ken. "In a Busy Year, Malcolm Jenkins Raised a Fist and Checked All the Boxes." *New York Times*, January 25, 2018.

Bondy, Filip. "Hodges Still Fights System." *New York Daily News*, December 11, 1996.

Bondy, Stefan. "Jason Collins Is Still Working to Give LGBTQ Pro Athletes a Voice." *New York Daily News*, June 28, 2019.

Boren, Cindy. "President Obama Remembers Muhammad Ali as a 'Man Who Shook up the World'." *Washington Post*, June 4, 2016.

Branch, John. "The Awakening of Colin Kaepernick." *New York Times*, January 7, 2019.

Brewer, Jerry. "Protesters Often Win History's Long Game: Ask Tommie Smith and John Carlos." *Washington Post*, October 20, 2018.

Brown, Jim. "Interview from Jail." *Sports Illustrated*, April 15, 2002.

Cart, Julie. "Asthma Is Joyner-Kersee's Toughest Foe." *Los Angeles Times*, June 6, 1991.

De la Cretaz, Britni. "Serena Williams's Tennis Outfits Defy the Sexist, Racist Norms Female Athletes Face." *Elle*, August 28, 2018.

DeSantis, Rachel. "Trump Criticizes Soccer Star Megan Rapinoe for Not Singing National Anthem after She Joined Colin Kaepernick's Protest." *People*, June 25, 2019.

Eig, Jonathan. "The Cleveland Summit and Muhammad Ali: The True Story." *The Undefeated*, June 1, 2017.

Eig, Jonathan. "The Real Reason Muhammad Ali Converted to Islam." *Washington Post*, October 26, 2017.

Folsom, Burton W. "Joe Louis vs. the IRS." *Mackinac Center for Public Policy Viewpoints*, July 7, 1997.

Hoffman, Benjamin, and Talya Minsberg. "The Deafening Silence of Colin Kaepernick." *New York Times*, September 4, 2018.

"Jackie Joyner-Kersee: Living with Asthma." *NIH Medline Plus*, Fall 2011.

Jackman, Jess. "For Closeted Gay Athletes, Endorsement Fears Persist." *Huffington Post*, February 19, 2017.

Jenkins, Malcolm. "What Protesting NFL Players Like Me Want to Do Next." *Washington Post*, September 30, 2017.

Korver, Kyle. "Privileged." *Players' Tribune*, April 8, 2019.

Mazique, Brian. "Michael Jordan: Did It Take 32 Years for His Airness to Gain an Appetite for Social Activism?" *Forbes*, July 26, 2016.

McDonald, Summer. "The Unexpected Legacy of Sheryl Swoopes." *ESPNW*, May 18, 2018.

Montague, James. "The Third Man: The Forgotten Black Power Hero." CNN, April 25, 2012.

Nelson, Amy. "Serena Williams, a Woman's Work and the Silence of Men." *Forbes*, September 9, 2018.

"Raised Fist: Tommie Smith and His 'Moment of Truth' at the 1968 Mexico City Olympics." *CBS News*, October 28, 2018.

Red, Christian. "Black Power Olympian Tommie Smith Tried to Mend Rift with Jesse Owens in Unanswered Letter." *New York Daily News*, February 20, 2016.

Rhoden, William. "Hodges Criticizes Jordan for His Silence on Issues." *New York Times*, June 5, 1992.

Root, Tik. "The Man Who Raised a Fist 50 Years Later." *The Atlantic*, October 2018.

Safdar, Khadeeja, and Andrew Beaton. "Nike Nixes 'Betsy Ross Flag' Sneaker after Colin Kaepernick Intervenes." *Wall Street Journal*, July 1, 2019.

Schmitz, Brian. "Sterling Controversy Hits Home for Doc, Kris Rivers." *Orlando Sentinel*, April 28, 2014.

Thomas, Louisa. "Political Football: Michael Bennett Wants NFL Players to Be a Force for Social Change." *New Yorker*, December 17, 2018.

Tsuji, Alysha. "D-Wade Gives $200K to 'March for Our Lives' Fundraiser." *USA TODAY*, March 10, 2018.

Venable, Cecilia Gutierrez. "The Texas Western Miners—1966." *Black Past*, February 28, 2016.

Vincent, Donovan. "The Forgotten Story Behind the 'Black Power' Photo from 1968 Olympics." *Toronto Star*, August 7, 2016.

Williams, Serena. "We Must Band Together to Fight for What's Fair." *Fortune*, March 8, 2019.

Wyche, Steve. "Colin Kaepernick Explains Why He Sat During National Anthem." *NFL Media*, August 27, 2016.

Yeboah, Kofie. "A Timeline of Events Since Colin Kaepernick's National Anthem Protest." *The Undefeated*, September 6, 2016.

Zirin, Dave. "Colin Kaepernick Was Mocked and Threatened for Taking a Knee. He's Also Winning." *The Nation*, October 19, 2017.

Author Interviews

Harvey Araton, Pete Babcock, A. Sherrod Blakely, Ron Borges, Rebekkah Brunson, Doris Burke, M. L. Carr, Mike Conley, Mike Connolly, Kyle Draper, Bill Fitch, Walt Frazier, Samuel Freedman, Matt Griffin, Tom Heinsohn, Johnette Howard, Kyrie Irving, Jason Jackson, Malcolm Jenkins, Roy S. Johnson, Mark Jones, Brevin Knight, Cedric Maxwell, Jack McCallum, Devin McCourty, George McGinnis, Robert Parish, Doc Rivers, Terry Rozier, Bob Ryan, Tom Sanders, Charles Scott, Mike Shalin, Tim Smith, Brad Stevens, Isiah Thomas, Dwyane Wade, Jerry West, Dominique Wilkins, Barry Wilner, and Matt Zeysing.

Other Interviews and Speeches

Kareem Abdul-Jabbar, in conversation with Bill Walton, Ann and Jerry Moss Theater, Santa Monica, California, 24 May 2017 (available on Vimeo and iTunes)

Kareem Abdul-Jabbar, on interviewing Martin Luther King Jr., *CBS This Morning*, April 3, 2018 (available on https://www.youtube.com/watch?v=fnl4fkrtouc)

John Carlos, "You Got 48 Hours" (available at https://www.youtube.com/watch?v=8jJJm-nh-2w)

Jason Collins speaks about coming out (available at https://www.youtube.com/watch?v=SOBn9ychoNI)

Magic Johnson talks business with Maverick Carter (available at https://www.youtube.com/watch?v=Fi1EkU9XB4E)

Jackie Joyner-Kersee speaks at the YWCA Annual Lunch 2012 (available at https://www.youtube.com/watch?v=JcvG5kSi4K4)

Jackie Robinson on the *Dick Cavett Show*, 1972 (available at https://www.youtube.com/watch?v=IwIwoYlIczM)

Bill Russell, interviewed by Taylor Branch on May 12, 2013, for the Library of Congress film archives (available at https://www.loc.gov/item/afc2010039_crhp0088/)

Sheryl Swoopes's Basketball Hall of Fame enshrinement speech (available at https://www.youtube.com/watch?v=4N2Q9WYsH0w)

ABOUT THE AUTHORS

BOB SCHRON has covered professional and collegiate sports for over forty years and is the author of several books, including *The Bird Era: A History of the Boston Celtics 1978–1988*. He has written for the Associated Press, *Bleacher Report*, and a number of professional team yearbooks and national magazines. Recipient of the President's Award from the Massachusetts Basketball Coaches Association, he has a master's degree in communication from The Ohio State University.

DEVIN McCOURTY is an NFL All-Pro free safety, and captain and three-time Super Bowl champion with the New England Patriots. He has a bachelor's degree in sociology from Rutgers University, and he is a voting member of the Task Force Board of the Players Coalition, a foundation established in 2017 by NFL players with the goal of "making an impact on social justice and racial equality at the federal, state, and local levels through advocacy, awareness, education, and allocation of resources."

INDEX

Index entries that refer to photo captions have page numbers set in italics.